Financially Fearless

Financially Fearless

———

*The LearnVest Program for
Taking Control of Your Money*

ALEXA VON TOBEL, CFP®

CROWN
BUSINESS

NEW YORK

All rights reserved.

Published in the United States by Crown Business, an imprint of the Crown Publishing Group, a division of Random House LLC, a Penguin Random House Company, New York.

www.crownpublishing.com

CROWN BUSINESS is a trademark and CROWN and the Rising Sun colophon are registered trademarks of Random House LLC.

Crown Business books are available at special discounts for bulk purchases for sales promotions or corporate use. Special editions, including personalized covers, excerpts of existing books, or books with corporate logos, can be created in large quantities for special needs. For more information, contact Premium Sales at (212) 572-2232 or e-mail specialmarkets@randomhouse.com.

Library of Congress Cataloging-in-Publication Data is available upon request.

ISBN 978-0-385-34761-7
Ebook ISBN 978-0-385-34762-4

Printed in the United States of America

Book design by Kristina Pyton
Illustrations on pages 1, 13, 19, 51, 69, 75, 97, 203, 227, 231, 269, 297, and 305 by Gavin Potenza
Chart illustrations by Fred Haynes

10 9 8 7 6 5 4 3 2 1

First Edition

To my mom and dad—
for allowing me to believe in
my wildest dreams,
and not for a moment
letting on that they were wild.

Financial planning shouldn't be a luxury.

Acknowledgments

Everything I do in life is a group effort, so there are many people to whom I am deeply grateful.

To my husband: Thank you for breathing belief in me as I started LearnVest four years ago. For holding my hand as I got the company off the ground and keeping me positive on my bad days. I look up to you and cannot imagine a day without you believing in me.

To my brothers: Thank you for teaching me to be tough and thus resilient enough to start LearnVest so millions of people across the country can have better lives. We were raised with a deep-seated desire to help others, and I am inspired by your putting that into practice as doctors. This is where my desire to help others comes from and I am so grateful to you both daily.

To John: I'll never forget the call that helped me take the leap out of business school. Thank you for believing in me enough to join me in this venture. I have had the most fun imaginable with you these last four years and cannot wait for the next many.

To my broader family, especially Tim and the Ryans: Thank you for everything. For reading everything published by and about LearnVest, for countless introductions, for the meals you've fed me to keep me going, and for letting me take naps or work on many occasions when I should have been elsewhere.

To my best friends: You all know who you are! Thank you for the daily laughs and for supporting me on this adventure.

I honestly feel blessed to have some of the most talented and savvy people around me—as my support and inspiration. I cannot imagine this journey without you all in my life.

To those who invested in LearnVest early: Thank you, John, Tom, Janet, Ben, Jeff, Jacki, Ann, Peter, Maria, Caryn, Craig, Ronald, David, Paul, Vinay, and Accel Partners, for seeing the problem and believing in our solution. And to our board—Ann, Theresia, and Lee—for your endless wisdom. By looking at LearnVest not only as an investment but also as a passion, you've helped lead our great movement.

To the tremendously talented LearnVest team: Thank you to everyone who touched and collaborated on this book. We are not just a company but a collection of passionate people. Criticism is better than compliments, and I appreciated all of yours. Special shout-outs to Ainslie, Kristina, Stephany, Ellen, Dimple, our entire edit team, our team of committed planners, and all of my early readers. Ada, thank you for translating my big ideas into words, and thank you for your research. And to Annie, who poured as much of her time and energy into this book as I did. My life would not run properly without you!

To our team at William Morris Endeavor: Thank you for supporting the LearnVest mission and seeing all the places we can go. Andy, Suzanne, Bethany, and Jason—you're the best. To our family at Sunshine Sachs—Dani, Jess, and Shawn. You've believed in our mission since day one and I truly have enjoyed every single day working with the three of you. At this point, you're family, and, Dani, you are a bright star!

And last but certainly not least, to the Crown team at Random House: Thank you for seeing that this is not just a book, but a needed movement. A movement that will empower Americans to live richer lives. Talia (my fearless editor!), Tara, Ayelet, Kimberly, Megan, Wade, Songhee, Chris, Phil, and Tina, thank you for seeing the future and believing in it with me.

Contents

Before we dive in, let's cross our t's and dot our i's.

We believe accurate, plain-English financial information should help you solve many of your own money problems. This book is designed to provide accurate and authoritative information with regard to the subject matter covered. But this text is not a substitute for personalized advice from a financial expert familiar with your specific financial circumstances. The advice contained herein may not be suitable for your particular situation, so you should consult with a professional where appropriate.

While the author has made every effort to provide accurate Internet addresses at the time of publication, the author does not assume any responsibility for errors or for changes that occur after publication. Further, the author does not have any control over and does not assume any responsibility for third-party websites or their content.

Neither the author nor the publisher shall be liable for any loss of profit or any other commercial damages, including but not limited to special, incidental, consequential, or other damages. The author and the publisher specifically disclaim any liability that a reader incurs from the use or application of the contents of this book. All "Fearless Tips" provided throughout this book are recommendations of the author or LearnVest.

LearnVest Program ("LearnVest Program" or "Advisor") is a registered investment advisor and subsidiary of LearnVest Inc. ("LearnVest Inc." or "Parent"). Many of the tools and resources mentioned

All good? Let's get started.

the

F

WORD

Why, hello there. I've got some good news. You've just taken the first step toward getting your finances in check.

Wait, come back here! I know what you're thinking. *What finances? Does this meek retirement account really need managing?* Or: *Here it comes; she's about to tell me to never go on vacation.* Or: *Give me a break, I don't have time to even think past lunch, let alone calculate interest compounding for thirty years.*

If you think financial planning isn't for you, think again. Financial planning is *not* just for the 1 percent. *Everyone* deserves the peace of mind that comes with having a good financial plan.

It doesn't matter how much money you do or don't have. Financial planning is not about getting rich; it's about *enriching* your life. While money doesn't buy happiness, it does buy security, stability, and the freedom to do the things that make life worth living, whether that means going back to school, starting a restaurant, buying a beach home, having a baby, going on a safari, or leaving a crappy relationship. Money is our lifeline.

When I first started writing this book, I wanted to call it *The F Word.* Why? Because talking about finances is still a *massive* taboo. We talk openly about everything else, from sex to diets to politics, yet when is the last time you spoke with your friends about money?

Well, in this book you better believe we're going to talk money, over and over again, from all different angles. We're going to take a hard, honest look at your spending and saving habits, and we're going to take a fine-tooth comb through your bank accounts and your wallet. **We're going to make money an issue, so *it becomes a nonissue.***

In this book I'm going to put you through the financial planning program I've developed in my years founding and running LearnVest, one of the leading online personal finance companies in the United States, and the LearnVest Program, a registered investment adviser that provides personal financial planning services. This Program is designed to help you earn better, save better, and spend better, so you can achieve the peace of mind that comes with knowing you are in *real* control of your finances. And a key component of the Program is openness—with others and with yourself.

By the time we're done here, you'll create a detailed, personalized financial plan tailored to how you *actually* live your life. In the process you'll get a clearer picture not only of what your money situation looks like now but also of where you'll be financially in twelve months, five years, even thirty years from now.

I want to give you that feeling of relief that comes with getting in control of your money—the relief that comes from not having to lie awake at night worrying about bills or credit-card payments, the relief that comes with knowing you have enough saved for tomorrow without having to sacrifice the things that bring you joy today.

Why *Not* Having a Plan *Is* a Plan—a Bad One

If this is the first time you're thinking about this stuff seriously, you might think you don't yet have a financial plan, but guess what? *Not* **having a plan** *is* **a plan—just a really, really bad one.** When you play it by ear, you're throwing away money that you *could* be spending on the things in life that really matter. Worse, by not making financial decisions you *are* in fact making decisions—ones that leave you vulnerable to scary blind spots that will hurt you down the line, like not having proper insurance. Winging it is no way to build the future of your dreams.

When I started out in personal finance, I believed I was the only one with oodles of "stupid" money questions. Then I realized that some of the smartest, most educated people I knew had similar questions. Despite all the books that have been written on the topic and all the financial experts out there touting their services, most people have no idea how to wade through the endless stream of conflicting and confusing advice online and on television, and who can blame us?

Most high schools and colleges and grad schools across the country do not teach you *anything* about it. I had a top-notch education and graduated having been taught diddly-squat about managing my money. How are we supposed to get off on the right foot when literally *no one* shows us how?

Not to mention that there's an endless amount of financial "stuff" to wade through—401(k)s, APRs, 529s, et cetera. It's easy to see why our nation has been struggling financially. How the heck is a normal person supposed to stay up to speed on all this stuff?

And with this confusion comes anxiety. Since founding LearnVest I have looked deep into the American financial psyche, and what I've found there is *worry*. Loads of it. I'm in the unique position of reading confessional e-mails from tens of thousands of LearnVest users on our free site. So I know what I'm talking about when I tell you that *most people* worry about money. Most people have doubts. Even those earning what the majority of Americans would consider to be a perfectly livable or even much more than livable salary are up at night worrying about money.

In poring through mountains of research, one thing I've found is that whether we're single or married, rich or poor, making $13 an hour or $300,000 a year, we all have the *exact* same questions about money: *Am I spending on the right things? Am I saving enough for my future? Am I making the best money decisions for me?*

The consequences of being in the dark about our finances are pretty scary: according to the American Payroll Association, more than two thirds of Americans are living paycheck to paycheck.[1] And I'm not just talking about people earning minimum wage. Three in ten Americans make more than $100,000 a year and *still* live paycheck to paycheck.[2] Clearly, having money doesn't mean you're immune to money stress. Not for nothing did Notorious B.I.G. coin "Mo Money Mo Problems."

And it's a vicious cycle: The less we know about money, the more stressed we feel about it. So we avoid dealing with it. And the more we avoid dealing with it, the more stressed we get, and so on into an infinity of sleepless nights.

But the good news is that no matter how much or how little money you have, you *can* manage it more strategically and put it to work for you. We *all* deserve that sense of freedom and power. We *all* can make progress.

I believe that **financial literacy is a fundamental human right.** That's why I started LearnVest: to give *everyone* the information and tools to take control of our financial futures, so we can finally stop feeling so alone and anxious about money. Before we get started, let me tell you more about why I got into the financial planning field in the first place and why I have devoted my life to blowing the lid off the money taboo.

Here's Why I Care So Much

When I was fourteen years old, my father passed away in an accident. I returned home from a fun summer night at the movies with friends to the worst news of my entire life. My mom, who was forty-eight at the time, was completely blindsided. In her twenty-five years of a very happy marriage she had never once imagined that she would find herself suddenly alone, caring for three children.

Not surprisingly, in the days that followed, we were all in paralyzing shock. Through the haze, I overheard my mom on the phone trying to better understand exactly where we had our financial accounts. On top of dealing with the most heart-wrenching, soul-shaking news she'd ever received, she also had to face another challenge: she would need to start dealing with our finances for the first time in her life.

It wasn't that my mom was incapable; far from it, actually. It was just that when my parents had originally split the household tasks (like most of America for the last century, I might add),[3] they had decided that my mom would manage the household budget and my dad the investments and long-term planning. As a result, there was my mom in the wake of his death also stressing over handling our money.

And that was when I vowed I would never, *ever*, let that happen to me. I made an unbreakable commitment to myself to learn everything I possibly could about my money. And I did. Upon graduating from college, I read every personal finance resource I could find, but nothing spoke to *me*—a smart person eager to establish a solid, 360-degree financial foundation. In the course of talking to my friends over the years and doing months of research, I realized I was not alone.

After a job in finance, I went back to Harvard for business school. Meanwhile, my business plan for LearnVest won a start-up competition, and after a lot of careful consideration, I took a leave of absence from business school to pursue my dream of helping millions of people with their money. My timing could not have been crazier: we were in the heart of the worst recession in eighty-one years and the world seemed to be crumbling around me. But I knew people were in need of money guidance more than ever.

In just four years, LearnVest has become a game-changer in the personal finance space. We've raised over $41 million in funding from investors who fundamentally believe in our mission. (They also backed Facebook, Etsy, and Kayak.) We've grown to be not only an award-winning website but also a financial planning company: the LearnVest Program has Certified Financial Planners™ and thousands and thousands of clients working together nationwide.

Today LearnVest is a *vast*, ever-growing community of smart, savvy people relying on our wealth of content and using our free Money Center tool (and supercool mobile app) to track their daily spending. Through the LearnVest Program, they are working with our experts to answer their money questions. We're making getting a financial plan as easy as getting a gym membership. All of our planners (myself included) carry the CFP® designation, which means they have loads of financial knowledge and experience. (I passed this test, too. It's a ten-hour, two-day exam.) We take this incredibly seriously and only work with the best. All in all, the LearnVest Program has been built for people who are taking charge of their finances and making their dreams reality. And by picking up this book, you've become one of them. Welcome!

How the LearnVest Program Works

At LearnVest, our motto is "Where Life Gets Richer," and I couldn't be more serious about these four little words. But we all have our own idea of what "rich" is. It's called *personal* finance for a reason; our relationships and our emotions are such a huge part of how and why we make and spend money. That's why when you're dealing with your money, it pays to ask yourself some very personal and sometimes uncomfortable questions, like: Are you intimidated by money? Do you *like* money? What is the worst-case money scenario that runs through your mind at 4:00 a.m.? How does money function in your relationships with other people?

That's why this book begins by walking you through a financial and psychological self-inventory; think of it as a therapy session for your finances. And it's why, along this journey, I'll share some inspiring stories and mortifying confessions that other brave people have shared with me. I want to show you that *you're not alone in this* and that there's strength in talking openly and honestly about money.

There's no reason we shouldn't add finances to the list of things we talk about over dinner with friends, or Gchat about with coworkers. I'm not saying you should host a "let's reveal our salaries and credit-card debt" party. What I am saying is that we *need* to talk to one another—our partners, our parents, and our kids—about money. That's why I want you to **share this book.** Read it alongside a spouse or pal, and make becoming financially fearless a thing to do *together*. At the end of the book you'll find tips on how you can form a LearnVest Club (which is like a book club, but more productive and powerful than discussing yet another historical novel).

Also, I realize that you may still have some questions when you're done with this book. That's why I'm making it possible for you to actually *talk* to a LearnVest Program expert if you want to. Keep track of your questions. (There are spaces in each section for you to write them down.) If there are any we don't answer in these pages, call us and we'll answer them on the phone. That's how serious I am about getting you a plan that works!

Talk to an LV *Expert*

This book will walk you through the LearnVest Program, and you'll come out on the other side with what I think is one of the greatest gifts we can give ourselves: a simple, easy-to-follow financial plan that *can* change your life.

It's a three-part process:

1. First we're going to figure out where you are right now, financially and psychologically. We're going to dive into your **money mind-set.** This isn't a fluffy exercise. We'll tell you why the way you *think* about your money matters and what role your past, present, and future play in your financial success and security (or lack thereof).

2. Next I'm going to introduce our favorite money-managing principle: the **50/20/30 rule.** Those numbers refer to the percentage breakdown of how

your take-home pay should be spent each month.[4] The 50 is for **essentials:** it includes your mortgage or rent payments, utilities, transportation to work, and groceries (not eating out). Essentials are the things you *literally* need to survive: a roof over your head, light and heat, a way of getting to work so you can earn an income, and food. The 20 is for the **future,** or your financial priorities: paying off debt (student loans, credit cards, etc.), building up an emergency savings fund, and saving for retirement. The remaining 30 is the fun part: **lifestyle.** That means all of the spending choices you make on a regular basis: eating out, taking vacations, going to the movies, and so on.

3 Finally I'm going to walk you through the steps you need to take to **protect yourself** so you can survive any financial storm. Curveballs are going to be thrown at you along this journey, and I'll show you how to protect yourself from life (shit happens), from the people around you (employers, family, friends), and even from yourself (bad habits that we're going to break).

In the course of this overhaul, we will talk about saving, but not in a crazy, unrealistic way. I'm not going to ask you to give up the things you love, and I'm not going to suggest you start buying your clothes at the dollar store (unless that's your jam) or turning in bottles and cans to make eighty cents—not when you can use the same time to call your credit-card company and save yourself hundreds of dollars in interest. When it comes to nickel-and-dime-level solutions, I believe your time on this earth is more valuable.

Yes, I'm going to share plenty of tips for saving money on things like rent and cell phone bills and travel, but I'm not going to go all extreme with the penny-pinching. **I won't tell you to do anything I wouldn't do myself.**

And yes, I will show you how to lower the APR on your credit cards in minutes, help you figure out how to painlessly pay off those student loans, and explain the simple things you need to do to make sure you're saving wisely for retirement. But what I'm not going to do is make your head spin with lots of talk about whether to invest in REITs or buy options. We're thinking macro here, people. We're not going to stick our fingers in a tiny crack in the dam if water is flooding over the banks.

So take the assessments. Fill out the worksheets and exercises. Make notes of your questions in the open spaces. Don't be afraid to write in the book and make it *yours*. If you're super-motivated, visit the companion website: www.learnvest.com /financiallyfearless. There you'll find even more problem-solving content. Finally, take advantage of our offer for a free financial consultation with a LearnVest Program expert. To schedule, simply go to the website (www.learnvest.com/financiallyfearless), and we'll connect you with an expert who can chat with you at *your* convenience.

Here. We. Go.

Now it's time to begin. We're going to get you on board with the LearnVest Program and start melting away any crummy financial anxiety. We're going to show you how to protect yourself, so that you can start sleeping better at night. **All situations can be improved;** even the worst money problems are livable and ultimately solvable. By the time you're done with this book, you'll look at personal finance in a way you never have before. My hope is that you'll finish this book not only with **a real plan** in your hand but also with a whole new outlook on money and the role it plays in your life. This is a plan that lets you be *you* . . . only richer. So grab a glass of wine—hell, grab a bottle—and let's get financially fearless together.

Our Commitment to
Your Money

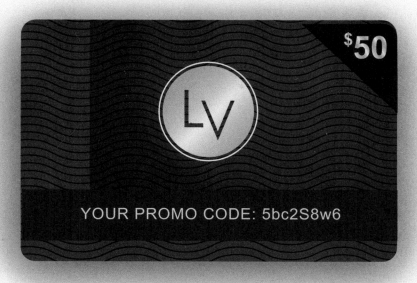

$50

YOUR PROMO CODE: 5bc2S8w6

— To redeem, go to —

LEARNVEST.COM/FINANCIALLYFEARLESS

You picked up this book for a reason: to make progress. As you create your financial plan, I want you to have your personal questions answered right away. That's why our team is at the ready to help you along the way. With this unique promo code, you'll have direct access to a complimentary phone consultation. If you want to keep working with a CERTIFIED FINANCIAL PLANNER™, we're giving you a $50 credit toward your custom Action Program. You're well on your way, and we can help you go the extra mile.

Learn More about our **ACTION**PROGRAM ≫

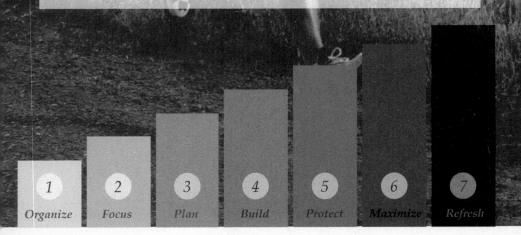

ACTIONPROGRAM »»

A 7-step program for your money.

Designed and customized for you.

1	2	3	4	5	6	7
Organize	Focus	Plan	Build	Protect	Maximize	Refresh

1 Organize
You get all your information in one secure place, so we know exactly where you're starting.

2 Focus
We help get you to a Net Zero budget, where you're spending on what matters most to you today (and tomorrow).

3 Plan
We cover the most critical parts of your financial security: retirement, debt, and basic savings.

4 Build
We help you protect your family and your stuff with the right insurance and estate documents.

5 Protect
We strategize on how to save up for big-ticket purchases and tell you how to optimize your loans.

6 Maximize
We recommend how your investment assets should be allocated. (No portfolio yet? We can get you started.)

7 Refresh
We're here as your life changes (for better or worse), and can always adapt your program to your new situation.

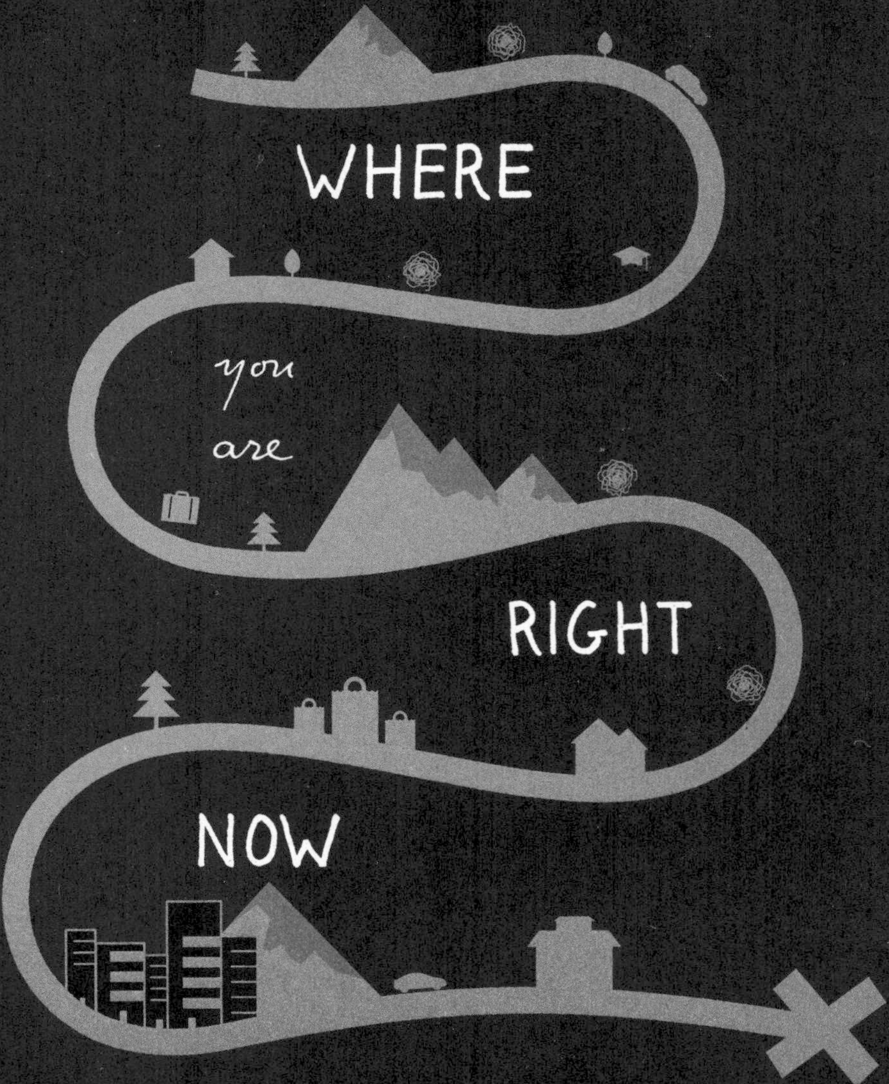
WHERE
you
are
RIGHT
NOW

In the next sections of this book, we're going to get your finances in shape down to the penny. But before we can know what your financial plan *should* look like, we need to figure out where you are—and perhaps more important, *who* you are now when it comes to money. Remember, personal finance is just that—personal—so if we want to whip you into the best financial shape of your life, we first need not only to look at what you spend and earn but also to get real about who you are and what you care about.

Every time we swipe our credit cards, we're making a statement about what we value in life. Do you like to splurge on vacations with friends? Do you stand in line overnight to buy the latest gadget? Does your rent bill snatch up 50 percent of your paycheck? Whether you're aware of it or not, each and every one of your financial decisions says something about you. **Ideally,** what you truly value correlates to how you're spending your money. Yet all too often we find ourselves throwing our money at stupid things we don't actually care about or even really notice. Luckily, the 50/20/30 plan is designed to change all that.

More good news: with the 50/20/30 plan, there's no judgment about spending *your* money the way *you* want to. You just have to take care of your financial future and immediate essentials first. At LearnVest, we recognize that money is a key to many (though certainly not all) of life's pleasures, so we believe that spending your money wisely means spending on the things in life that you value.[1]

I grew up with two different money mind-sets. On one side

I had my chic paternal grandparents living in Europe. They passed on the "von" in my name and a love of the finer things in life. On the other side I had my down-to-earth maternal grandparents in South Bend, Indiana, who passed on a sense of frugality.

What about you? What values, bad or good, did you inherit regarding money? Let's look at that question more closely.

Therapy Sesh

Now it's your turn. I want you to think hard about three things:

1 How you *feel* about money

2 What you *do* with your money

3 What your *plans* are for your money

Be honest with yourself here. (It's not always easy!) As you fill out the worksheets in this section, try to dig a little deeper into your financial subconscious. Don't hold back. **Remember, this is a judgment-free zone.**

Exploring your past, present, and future will give you a sense of your money personality and your financial strengths and weaknesses. Think of this section as a Myers-Briggs™ personality test for your money. Why bother going through this exercise? Because your money personality is the **key** to understanding and letting go of any guilt you may have about past mistakes, so you can begin to grow and change.

Financial psychologist Brad Klontz (the fact that such a specialty exists is telling, isn't it?) says that a lot of us believe that our negative financial behavior is a result of our having poor will-power, being stupid, or being lazy. But it's not true.[2] The way we deal with money is more often than not psychological—a reaction to money patterns we experienced growing up. We all have some hang-ups. By the end of this chapter you will have a better sense of what your hang-ups about money are, where they came from, and where there's room for you to improve. Think about it this way: knowing *why* you're doing what you're doing doesn't always guarantee overnight change, but *not* knowing is a surefire way to keep making the same mistakes over and over forever.

Here are the three things we're going to talk about:

1. **Past.** What role did money play in your childhood? How did your past form your fundamental beliefs about money?

2. **Present.** What do your financial actions say about you? If you took a snapshot of your financial situation right now, what would it look like? What are your money habits?

3. **Future.** Where do you see yourself going, and what will it take financially to get there? What do you dream about for your future? What do you want most in life? It's time to identify and prioritize your goals, so you can begin working to make them a reality.

GROUNDWORK

your money mind-set

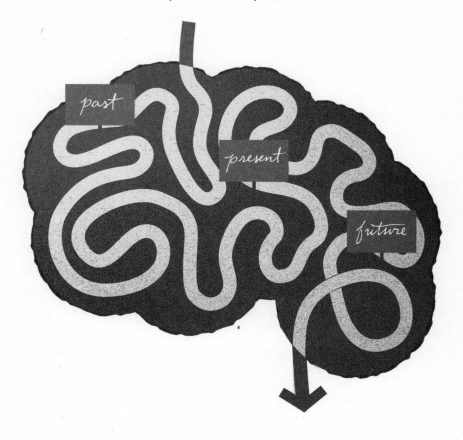

The Past: Where You've Been

In this section we are going to figure out the answer to this deceptively simple question: Do you innately believe money is good or evil? To answer this question, we have to look at what's lying below the surface. What's your gut telling you? Do you think money is the way to happiness, or the root of all trouble? Do you secretly believe money is your birthright, or do you silently worry you don't deserve it? Do you like thinking about it, or does it make you anxious?

A groundbreaking study identified four core money beliefs, established at childhood, that drive our financial behavior and habits.[1] The study explained that these subconscious beliefs, often shaped by our parents and early childhood memories, become the lens through which we approach our finances throughout our adult lives.

So let's get to the bottom of your money foundation. It can be a little tough to open up about this, but remember, we're in this together! Throughout this section I'll share some of my own money psychology with you.

Your First Money Memory

According to Klontz, our earliest money memories will shape our feelings about money and determine how comfortable or uncomfortable we are dealing with our finances as adults.[2] Think back to yours. Maybe it was finding a few coins in the couch and hiding them from your siblings, your grandmother slipping you a twenty, or your parents asking you to order the cheapest thing on the menu.

What's your earliest money memory?

↙ Write it down

_____

_____

_____

_____

_____

FEARLESS LESSON   *Why It Matters*

Your money beliefs are, according to finance experts Brad and Ted Klontz[3]:

- Developed in childhood
- Often passed down from generation to generation in family systems
- Typically unconscious

A recent article in the *American Journal of Family Therapy* explains that "money is used to control children, punish estranged spouses, measure a person's true feelings, buy freedom from relationships, or stop a partner from leaving. . . . We invented money and we use it, yet we cannot either understand its laws or control its actions. It has a life of its own which it properly should not have."[4]

MONEY MIC: *Alexa's First Money Memory*

My earliest money memory is from when I was about five years old. We had these great little books like Who Is Johnny Appleseed? *My dad would say, "If you can read this book in a day— twenty-four hours—I will pay you ten dollars" (which seemed like a fortune then). These were dauntingly long books, sixty pages! But I loved the challenge and so I would do it. And then I would get the money. I learned that money was something you earned if you worked really hard and that I loved that feeling, of doing something difficult and then reaping the rewards. Later I realized that my parents were probably very shrewdly getting me to sit still for a full day, and $10 was just very cheap babysitting! Ultimately, I'm happy they did it. It left me feeling that money was the result of hard work.*

Your Parents' Attitudes About Money

When you were growing up, your parents were your direct—and often only—source of information about money. So it's only natural that their attitudes, behaviors, and beliefs would in some way rub off.

We can't pick our families, but we do have control over how our families and our upbringings affect our grown-up lives. And we can choose to emphasize the good that we got from our families rather than the not-so-good. In my case, entrepreneurship is one of the best things that runs in my family, and I have embraced it.

How did your family handle money when you were a child? How did family members talk to you and one another about money? Or was money ignored? I've heard it *all* before: from the stepdad with a gambling addiction to the mom telling her daughter to keep recently purchased clothes a secret from her dad to the father who sat his young child down with the *Wall Street Journal* to review investments.

Did your parents talk to you frequently about money? Did they give you an allowance and explain the benefits of saving? Just get it off your chest.

Write about your parents' relationship to money.

↙ Write it down

_____

_____

_____

_____

Your Parents' Money Motto

Another way to think about your family's attitudes toward money is to try to remember if there's a certain saying or phrase about money that they often used. Examples include: "Save for a rainy day, and there's *always* a rainy day" and "It takes money to make money." Chances are that even if you don't *agree* with whatever statement was commonly thrown around your childhood home, it is still a voice that pops into your head.

My parents always said, "It's only money," meaning life isn't just about money. That's why I grew up believing that money alone won't make me happy.

Write your family's most memorable motto here.

↙ Write it down·

FEARLESS LESSON | *Why It Matters*

If your parents took the time to teach you about money, you're in luck! Turns out, there is a correlation between extensive money-management education in childhood and higher credit scores and lower credit-card debt in adulthood.[5] Plus, the quality of financial education in childhood is an accurate predictor of a child's "financial, psychological and personal well-being" as he or she grows.[6]

MONEY MIC: *What Is Your First Money Memory?*

When I was ten, I went to work with my dad. He paid me $1 per hour for my work. Then he made me give him $3 for gas money, and I had to pay for my own Coke when we went out to have a drink after. —Kathy, 36, Chicago, IL

My first memory of money is when my parents gave me my first piggy bank. It was actually in the shape of a dog. After they explained its purpose, I fell in love with the idea. I stashed my bank in a corner of my closet, so my little brother would stop stealing my allowance money. —David, 46, Atlanta, GA

When I was about eight, I remember watching my mother write a check at her desk and I asked her what she was doing. She explained that the check was just like money. I was so confused. I didn't understand how she could "write" money for any amount she wanted. I had no idea that she actually needed to have cash in the bank to cover the amount of the check!

—Laurie, 44, San Diego, CA

I was telling my dad about how I was going to have a lemonade stand, and that I'd put money in the payment jar up front so other people would think, "Hey, lots of other people have already bought this; it must be good." My dad laughed so hard, but in a way that I knew I'd hit on something "grown-up." I couldn't have been more than five or six. —Caitlin, 26, Austin, TX

 MONEY MIC: *What Alexa's Parents Taught Her About Money:*

My father, a doctor, would tell me at the age of ten exactly how much was in my college savings account. And every summer I had a job. My dad ran a private practice, so some of my first jobs were working in his doctor's office, where he took care of patients with autism, and he paid me so I could contribute to my savings. I felt like he helped me be thoughtful about money, simply because we talked about it.

My siblings and I often joke that at the holidays, we'd open up a box and find Costco socks. My mom is the best saver you've ever met. She grew up in a very frugal household herself and carried that forward. Instead of Keds, we'd have "Peds," or whatever the heck the generic version was called, even though the brand-name shoes were only a difference of $5. But we would take trips to Europe, where my grandparents lived. My mom would save on *the things that she believed were unnecessary, like us having cool shoes, so we could do what she thought was essential: seeing the world. Now, I'd have to say I agree with my mom's method!*

All that said, despite my parents passing on good values, I still had countless questions about money later on—hence, why I started LearnVest and became a CFP®.

Now that we've taken the time to think through how your parents acted around money, let's look at how these messages shaped your beliefs and attitudes. Based on your upbringing, are you positively or negatively oriented toward money? Do you fundamentally believe money is good or evil? Are you scared of it? Obsessed with it? Angry at it?

You Believe Money Is a Source of Happiness

If this is you, you tend to believe money can solve your problems. You see money as the positive reward for hard work and as a tool that can be used to elevate your life. Simply put, you think money makes life easier. While money doesn't conjure up a dark storm cloud for you (which is a good thing), there are some potential pitfalls if this is your attitude. For example, you may gamble (in an effort to put your money to work for you) or overspend (in an effort to get the most out of your dollar). You may also be obsessive about money. When money becomes *the* filter through which you make every decision, and you're giving it tons of emotional value, you can be tempted to spend too much on the wrong things. Or, on the flip side, an obsession with money can make you cheap. Yes, there is such a thing as being too cheap! At the end of the day, you need **balance** in your financial life, just as you do in your diet.

If you fall into this category you will shine in the "20" chapter, where we address your future. You likely already have a vision of the dream life money can buy, so this chapter will help you focus on the *exact* steps you'll need to take to get there. You should also pay particular attention to the concept of "cost per happy" in the "30" chapter. There I'll show you exactly how to quantify the positive value of money in your day-to-day life. As you read on, take note of ways you can leverage your positive attitude about money to maximize your wealth.

You Believe Money Is a Source of Stress

If this is you, money may have been a source of drama and tension in your childhood. (If it was, know you're **definitely not** alone there. We've all experienced some of that.) So now, even as an adult, you may cringe every time money comes up. You may feel like you'll never have enough, so why even try? Or you feel like having too much is a problem in and of itself. As a result, you may handle money by just not dealing with it. Bad behavior may show up in the form of missing payments, excessive aversion to any financial risk, being too cheap, or being overly private about your finances.

If this is you, first, give yourself a clean slate. Tell yourself everything will be okay. As my parents would say, "It's *only* money." As you read on, you will learn that money is not inherently good or bad. It is *simply* a tool—one that can be used either well or badly. If you have the core belief that money is bad, you should pay particular attention to the "50" chapter on essentials, as you may need extra help setting up a balanced budget. Plus, keeping your essential expenses in check will give you some freedom to actually *enjoy* the benefits that money can buy elsewhere in your life. Also focus on the chapter "Protect Yourself from Others." If money has created problems in past or current relationships, you may be able to use these tips on better communicating your financial position—with everyone from your landlord to your significant other.

The Present: Your Behavior

Now that we've taken some time to reflect on the core money beliefs that come out of your past experiences, we're going to bring it back to the present and explore your current financial behavior and habits.

Believe it or not, we make about *six to ten money decisions every day.* These decisions are guided by habits both conscious and unconscious, both good and bad. We all have money habits we'd like to change. But we have to be aware of what those bad ones are if we're going to change them. For example, most of us have stores where we habitually overspend. Mine are One Kings Lane and Target.

Our financial present isn't shaped by any one big thing. It's a result of a series of many microdecisions, driven by our own money personalities. If you can figure out why you're making the microchoices you are, you can figure out how to rewire yourself to make better ones.

Here are three of the most common bad habits I see in people:

1. Denial

Two Hebrew University researchers observed that people often deliberately look away from money problems—specifically, investing problems—in the hope that doing so will make those problems disappear. They call this "the ostrich effect."[7] Are you failing to budget? Are you in the dark about your credit score? Are you ignoring how you'll pay for your kids' college? Not saving the suggested amount for retirement? It may be time to get your head out of the sand.

2. Impulsiveness

Do you rush into financial decisions? Managing your money well takes thought and, of course, **advance planning.** It's okay to splurge once in a while, but being impulsive can really hurt your bottom line. Whenever you're making a big purchase or committing a lot of money to something, make sure to sleep on it first.

"Carpe diem" is generally awesome life advice, but it can be *terrible* financial advice. It essentially equates to using tomorrow's money to pay for today. Some of the hallmarks of the living-only-for-today bad habit: Keeping all your cash in a checking account. Not saving for retirement. Not making a will. Not having enough insurance. These are all signs that you're sabotaging your future in order to get by in the here and now.

Sometimes a lack of planning for the future is rooted in uncomfortable feelings about getting older. Economics and psychology professor George Loewenstein sees an "empathy gap" in people's relationships with their future selves. "The empathy gap tends to promote undersaving," he explains, "because we can't imagine either the pleasures of an affluent retirement or the pains of a lean one."[8] C'mon, start imagining yourself in your future-you shoes already!

3. The Joneses

Are you always comparing yourself to others who have more—your friends, your neighbors, your coworkers, even strangers?

Listen, *everyone* has some of this. But if I let myself constantly compare my decisions to those of others, I may never feel good about another decision again. At some point, we all need to learn to be fulfilled with what we *do* have, with the goals we *have* accomplished, and with the bright future that awaits us. (And I already think you're fabulous for picking up this book and caring about yourself!)

If you don't recognize yourself or your behavior in these three descriptions, great! But you aren't totally out of the woods yet. At LearnVest, we see people every day with all kinds of self-defeating money habits. Here are twenty. Check the ones that apply to you. Then go back and star the ones that give you the most trouble. We're going to refer back to this list later in the book when we talk about how to protect ourselves from our own worst habits.

Twenty Typical Bad Money Habits

- [ ] Carrying a credit-card balance month to month.
- [ ] Assuming that you're too young or too old to start investing for the future.
- [ ] Keeping all of your money in a checking account.
- [ ] Being reckless with your personal information. Giving out your Social Security number without having confirmed that it is absolutely necessary.
- [ ] Impulse shopping.
- [ ] Not asking for a raise when you deserve one.
- [ ] Borrowing money from friends and family.
- [ ] Ignoring your student loans.

- [ ] Taking money out of a retirement account.
- [ ] Making late payments.
- [ ] Not budgeting.
- [ ] Not knowing your credit score.
- [ ] Dipping into an emergency fund for nonemergencies. (Having nothing to wear is not an emergency!)
- [ ] Avoiding writing a will.
- [ ] Not saving a set amount automatically out of every paycheck.
- [ ] Not having enough or the right insurance: health, life, renter's, homeowner's, car, etc.
- [ ] Trying to keep up with the Joneses when you can't afford to.
- [ ] Not taking advantage of employer benefits like 401(k) matching or a flexible spending account.
- [ ] Paying bills by snail mail.
- [ ] Living beyond your means (most commonly, spending too much on housing).

In the course of my research, three *good* habits have emerged that, more than any others, predict people's success with money: organization, thoughtfulness, and independent thinking. These are *the* most important things to understand about yourself. They help explain what's driving your behavior and what may be at the root of any problems you're having.

Where people fall on the spectrum in these three categories shows how secure they are with money and how likely they are to succeed in reaching their financial goals. So do the following mini exercises and think hard about where you fall.

Spectrum 1: Organization

Here's what organization looks like. Check those that apply to you.

- ☐ You know how much you have in your accounts. (1 point)
- ☐ You have your payments automated so they are never late. (1 point)
- ☐ You know your credit score. (1 point)
- ☐ You have a budget. (1 point)
- ☐ You have calendar alerts set up on your phone or e-mail. (1 point)
- ☐ You have your bills in one place, as in a dedicated Gmail account. (1 point)
- ☐ You have all the insurance you and your dependents need. (1 point)

Where do you fall on the spectrum between organized and disorganized? Add up all your points and mark your results here.

```
  0     1     2     3     4     5     6     7
◄───┼─────┼─────┼─────┼─────┼─────┼─────┼───►
```

Disorganized (0 points)   *Organized (7 points)*

If you scored high on the organization spectrum, congratulations. But guess what? There are still ways to get even *more* organized, like adopting the 50/20/30 method for your budget (which I'll walk you through in the next section). And if you got a low mark, that 50/20/30 budget is going to come in even more handy, because it's going to prevent you from throwing away hundreds of dollars each year thanks to thoughtless spending, forgotten bills, and missed deductions.[9]

If you clocked in at disorganized, you need to do a little prep work before we even get started on 50/20/30. Automate your bills. Set up recurring contributions to your retirement accounts. Take a daily Money Minute (more on this later) to track your spending. Here are a few tips to help you get your new organized self in gear.

Set Calendar Reminders for Your Financial To-dos

1 **Your bills.** Make sure that you set calendar reminders for payments and bills that occur at regular intervals—not just monthly but throughout the year, like memberships, magazine subscriptions, vet visits, gifts, vacations, and insurance premiums.

2 **Your savings.** Make yourself a bill! Automate your savings for any special goals, plus your retirement savings, and set a calendar reminder to pop up whenever they'll come out of your checking account. This should happen at the beginning of the month, so you make sure to do it.

3 **Your taxes.** If you're a freelancer, a small business owner, or self-employed, remember to set up quarterly tax payments. And no matter what your employment status, you should always block out time to finish your taxes in January and February (*not* on April 14).

4 **Credit score checks.** Set reminders to review your score at CreditKarma.com every month, and get a credit report free every four months from one of the three credit bureaus—TransUnion, Equifax, and Experian—via AnnualCreditReport.com.

5 **Your health.** Find out when your insurance company offers open enrollment and when you're due for physicals, dental checkups, and the like. Schedule them in advance so you don't forget.

How to Automate

Some finance experts will tell you to actively pay your bills, be-cause it forces you to pay attention to how much you're spending. Others will say you should automate everything and not think about it. After a ton of thought, I am now pro-automation, be-cause there are so many other phenomenal ways to track your spending. It's not worth the time to go online every single time your bill is due. Plus, we all lead such busy, fast-paced lives that if we don't automate our regularly recurring payments, the risk of missing a due date is too high. Late payments could mean late fees and hurting your credit score. There is a big caveat, though: **automating your bills is *not* an excuse to stop *reading* your bills.** You should still be sure to carefully check your bills every month so you know exactly how much is being withdrawn.

Here are a couple of ways to simplify this review process:

1. **Set up reminders** on your calendar of choice (I'm a Google Calendar fan) so you know exactly when your bills will hit.

2. **Create a separate e-mail account** just for your financial statements (e.g., alexasbills@gmail.com) and make sure to check it regularly to ensure that nothing slips through the cracks.

Isn't it nice to know that there are some money mishaps you can avoid, just with some simple organization?

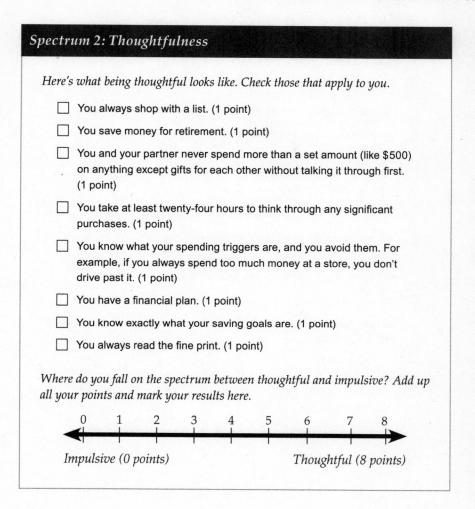

Spectrum 2: Thoughtfulness

Here's what being thoughtful looks like. Check those that apply to you.

☐ You always shop with a list. (1 point)

☐ You save money for retirement. (1 point)

☐ You and your partner never spend more than a set amount (like $500) on anything except gifts for each other without talking it through first. (1 point)

☐ You take at least twenty-four hours to think through any significant purchases. (1 point)

☐ You know what your spending triggers are, and you avoid them. For example, if you always spend too much money at a store, you don't drive past it. (1 point)

☐ You have a financial plan. (1 point)

☐ You know exactly what your saving goals are. (1 point)

☐ You always read the fine print. (1 point)

Where do you fall on the spectrum between thoughtful and impulsive? Add up all your points and mark your results here.

0   1   2   3   4   5   6   7   8

Impulsive (0 points)   *Thoughtful (8 points)*

If you landed on the impulsive side of the spectrum, make a rule for yourself that you'll sleep on every major decision for at least one night and consider at least two choices seriously for every purchase.

Studies have shown that people with "shorter time horizons" are more prone to racking up debt,[10] so if you build in a time buffer you'll be ahead of the game. You can also set up debit- and credit-card alerts for when you exceed a certain threshold of spending. These simple reminders will help keep that impulsive demon at bay.

Spectrum 3: Independent Decision Making

Here's what being independent looks like. Check those that apply to you.

- ☐ You consult objective experts when making big decisions. (1 point)
- ☐ You don't do something just because everyone else is doing it. (1 point)
- ☐ If a salesman tries to talk you into something you don't *really* want, you say you'll need to think about it. (1 point)
- ☐ You recognize that your personal finances are unique. (1 point)
- ☐ You realize the grass is always greener—but you don't let it get to you. (1 point)
- ☐ You consider yourself to be pragmatic. (1 point)
- ☐ You set goals for yourself based on your current situation. (1 point)
- ☐ You feel confident in your ability to make decisions—once you've done your research. (1 point)

Where do you fall on the spectrum between dependent and independent? Add up all your points and mark your results here.

```
 0   1   2   3   4   5   6   7   8
```

Dependent (0 points)   *Independent (8 points)*

If you are finding yourself constantly comparing your money to your peers', some psychologists suggest you may want to switch up your social circle.[11] Or, more practically, you could remind yourself that personal finance is not a competitive sport.

Wrapping Up

If you completed all the exercises above, give yourself a hand. You've made a huge stride toward owning your issues and becoming more self-aware about your financial behavior. Are you an organized-thoughtful-independent type, or a disorganized-impulsive-dependent type? Wherever you fall, know that your present self isn't a life sentence! I'm going to help you take action. Throughout the book, and particularly in the chapter on protecting yourself from life, I'm going to help you say *sayonara* to those bad habits. You can always evolve and change, especially if you know where you want to go, the subject of the next section.

The Future: Where You're Going

Your present and future are always at odds with each other. You want to spend money today, but your future self wants you to sock it away so future you can spend it on a trip with the grandkids. It helps to picture the future you—just a more adorable, more vulnerable, slightly more wrinkled version of your current self, of course—so that you care about what happens to this older you and keep him or her in mind when you're going about your financial life now.

Visualizing not just your future self but also your future goals can be incredibly powerful. One sports psychology study showed how visualization could in some cases replace practicing. One group of basketball players in the study practiced free throws every day. Another made free throws just on the first and last day but spent twenty minutes a day visualizing free throws. The visualizers improved almost exactly as much as the practicing group.[12] I've experienced this firsthand: When I was in college, I was on the varsity diving team. The dive itself took just seconds, but I spent days visualizing beforehand. Every time I did, it made me less nervous and more confident.

A recent study also showed that when people wrote down their goals, they were significantly more likely to achieve them.[13]

The point is that the following exercises are not frivolous or just here for fun. These exercises are meant to help you **visualize the future you want (and give you an outlet to put it in writing)** so we can look at what you need to do to **get there**.

FEARLESS LESSON   *How to Talk About Goals*

Life coaches are all about setting goals. Here's some of the best advice I've seen[14] about how to discuss goals in a way that makes them achievable:

1. Write goals in the first person and present tense: "I have $50,000 in savings."

2. Use specific numbers and a specific time line: "I have a salary of $100,000 at the age of 35."

3. Use specific, positive language: "I live in sunny Los Angeles" (as opposed to negative language: "I no longer live in the Northeast in that hideously cramped apartment").

4. Imagine your future in at least three areas, like personal ("I am married"), career ("I am a vice president"), and health ("I work out every other day").

5. Think about what your ideal future environment is like. "I live within 10 miles of my two best friends. I live on a quiet, tree-lined street." Or: "I live in a loft in the heart of downtown."

In Ten Years . . .

Now let's do a little exercise that reminds me of a game called MASH, which you may have played as a kid. What will you be doing in ten years? Remember that this is a visualization exercise, so write your answers in the present tense.

Share your vision for your FAMILY life.

Are you happily married? Happily single? Do you have a herd of rambunctious children running around? Are you relishing the quiet of being an empty nester?

↙ Write it down

_____

_____

_____

_____

What does your future HOME look like?

If you're artistically inclined, draw it here. Picket fence? Landscaped gardens? Wood-burning pizza oven? Renovated loft? Infinity pool?

↙ Draw it here

Share your vision for your CAREER.

Do you work? What's your title? What's your favorite thing about what you do?

↙ Write it down

_____

_____

_____

_____

_____

Share your vision for your MONEY.

↙ Write it down

How much is in your emergency savings fund?

_____

Your retirement savings?

_____

How much is your home worth, and what's your mortgage?

_____

How much credit-card debt do you have?

_____

How much student-loan debt do you have?

_____

What's your salary?

_____

What's your significant other's salary (if applicable)?

_____

When you splurge, what's it on (clothes, meals, presents)?

_____

Where do you go on vacation (Greece, Mount Rainier, Austin)?

_____

How are you getting around (Prius, private jet, city bus)?

_____

When you're sixty-five . . . ↙ Fill it out

It's a Wednesday in June, and you're sixty-five. Imagine what your day looks like. Fill in the blanks to craft your vision.

I wake up at ____ a.m. I live in ________, and I'm happy to be here because ________. Today is a ________ (busy/relaxing/average?) day. I look in the mirror and my reflection is ________.

I spend my morning ________. Then it's off to ________, where I ________. In the afternoon, I ________.

Throughout the day, I spend time with some of my favorite people: ________, ________, and ________. As the day winds down/picks up, I ________. My head hits the pillow at ____ p.m. I can't wait for tomorrow, when I'll ________.

Add more details here:

____

____

____

____

____

____

____

____

____

____

____

____

MONEY MIC: *Me at Sixty-Five*

LearnVest's Chief Strategy Officer shares her hopes and dreams:

When I am sixty-five, I want to be walking down the streets of New York (where I live), Toronto (where I grew up), or Paris (oh why not?) with my husband. We will have just finished a wonderful lunch. I will be dressed in a fashionable outfit, with a great haircut. I will have let my hair go gray (maybe . . . still debating that one). I want to have a clear vitality about me. You know those people who just look great? The ones who look well rested and stress free? I want to be that person.

As I am walking, I will get a few phone calls. One will be from my secretary letting me know that the meeting for the board of directors that I sit on is confirmed for next month. Another will be from my youngest daughter, letting me know she passed her final exams with flying colors. Yet another from my oldest daughter saying that she will see us at the cottage this weekend with her husband and kids and finally one from my son, just checking in as he so often does.

This vision embodies absolutely everything I hold to be important in my life. I will be with my husband in what will then be our thirty-fourth year of marriage. I will be successful and respected in my career. And I will have a strong relationship with each of my children and their families.

So how does this vision impact my life today? Well, it affects me every single day. I make moment-by-moment decisions paying homage to that woman walking down the street. I do assume with almost 100 percent certainty that I won't achieve that full vision. Life takes some wicked turns, and no matter how carefully I map it out, many things will not happen as I imagine. But it is so much easier to get close to our fantasy life if we have a plan.

—Ainslie, 42, Larchmont, NY

What Will Your Dream Life Cost?

Now that you've visualized the life of your dreams, this worksheet will help you estimate how much you'll need to live it.

This isn't a scientific, inflation-adjusted, down-to-the-decimal-place estimate of your expected expenses up until the time you retire (after all, I'm not a fortune-teller). But I have provided some ballpark numbers of common expenses below, so you can illustrate how much your big-ticket expenses in future years *might* cost you.

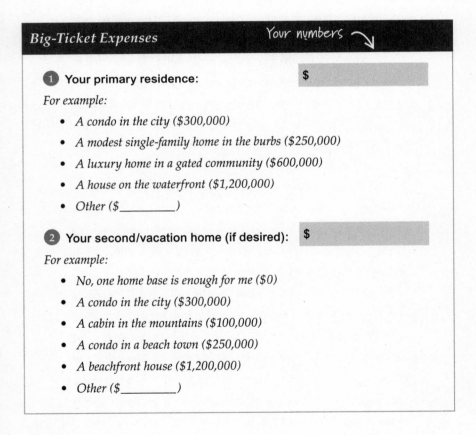

Big-Ticket Expenses   Your numbers

1 Your primary residence: $

For example:

- *A condo in the city ($300,000)*
- *A modest single-family home in the burbs ($250,000)*
- *A luxury home in a gated community ($600,000)*
- *A house on the waterfront ($1,200,000)*
- *Other ($_____)*

2 Your second/vacation home (if desired): $

For example:

- *No, one home base is enough for me ($0)*
- *A condo in the city ($300,000)*
- *A cabin in the mountains ($100,000)*
- *A condo in a beach town ($250,000)*
- *A beachfront house ($1,200,000)*
- *Other ($_____)*

3 **Your vehicle:** $

For example:

- *Toyota Prius or similar ($25,000)*
- *Mini Cooper or similar ($30,000)*
- *Ford Expedition or similar ($40,000)*
- *BMW X6 or similar ($60,000)*
- *Range Rover or similar ($90,000)*
- *None; I'll ride my bike! ($0)*
- *Other ($_____)*

- -

Sum of big-ticket expenses: $

Family Expenses *Your numbers* ↘

4 **Your children:** $

Multiply the number of children you have/want by $234,900—the average cost of raising a child to the age of eighteen.

5 **Your child-care costs:** $

*For example (costs reflect the **first five years** of your child's life):*

- *My partner or I will stay at home to raise them. ($0)*
- *My parents live nearby—free babysitting! ($0)*
- *We both work and will need a nanny. ($150,000)*
- *I'll work part-time and use day care on those days. ($90,000)*

Don't forget to multiply by the number of children!

6 Your child's college education: $

For example (costs reflect all years of school):

- *State school ($90,000)*
- *Private school ($200,000)*
- *Community college ($6,000)*
- *Will use 100 percent student loans/scholarships/financial aid ($0)*

Don't forget to multiply by the number of children!

. . . .

Sum of family expenses: $

Ongoing Expenses   Your numbers

7 Your activities (per year): $

For example:

- *Reading books, walking, and enjoying hobbies ($0)*
- *Pursuing hobbies (karate, photography, learning Italian) and going out for dinners and drinks ($10,000)*
- *Hanging out at home: gardening, puttering, hosting casual dinners with friends ($5,000)*
- *Eating out at the finest restaurants, sailing, and attending galas ($25,000)*

8 Your spending (per year): $

For example:

- *I love shopping but always search for a deal. ($8,000)*
- *I'm low maintenance . . . most of the time. ($4,000)*
- *I'm all about high quality and high fashion. ($20,000)*
- *I'm a minimalist. ($2,000)*

⑨ **Your travel (per year):** $

For example:

- *Frequent trips to exotic places like Bali ($15,000)*
- *Twice a year, abroad and domestically ($5,000)*
- *Almost never, but always in a car when I do! ($1,000)*
- *Twice a year, mostly domestically ($2,000)*

Annual sum of ongoing expenses: $

Multiply this by the number of years between now and retirement (normal retirement age is sixty-seven): $

What will your dream life roughly cost? Your number ↘

Add up the sum boxes from the last three pages: $

The examples above are estimated costs based on 2013 general expenses nationwide.

Keep this number and this self-inventory in mind as you start working to make your fantasy life happen. **My dream for the future you is that you get to where you want to be and beyond.** It's about putting the time in *now*, so you can make sure money doesn't stand in your way.

Okay, so we've dug deep into your past, taken a long, hard look at your present, and identified what you want for the future. Now we're going to get down to the nitty-gritty of your current financial picture. First let's look at what you've accomplished.

What You've Accomplished

✓   Established your core money value: good vs. evil

✓   Given yourself a clean slate if you need it

✓   Considered how your earliest money memories and your parents' attitudes about money influenced you

✓   Identified your day-to-day money habits

✓   Set up calendar alerts for major money milestones

✓   Set up your account on LearnVest's Money Center and downloaded our free apps

✓   Created clear goals for your future family, home, career, and financial life

✓   Envisioned a day in your life at age sixty-five

✓   Calculated what your dream life could roughly cost you

Questions for Your Expert

If you still have questions about anything we've covered in this section, write them here and then go to www.learnvest.com/financiallyfearless for answers.

I still don't understand . . .

_____

_____

Where do I find . . .

_____

_____

Talk to an
LV
Expert

What should I do about my . . .

_____

_____

Examples:

My ideal career seems out of reach right now. What should I do to get on the fast track?

My parents passed on some pretty bad money habits, and I'm still not sure how to talk to them about money—even as an adult. Where do I start?

The estimated sum of my dream life is sky high. Is that number within reach or do I need to reconsider my priorities and reset my expectations?

RUNNING
your
NUMBERS

By examining your feelings (and sticking with me through that barrage of nosy questions), you've just taken the first step toward becoming financially fearless. The second step is about where you stand today (numbers-wise).

In this section, I'm going to take you through all of the financial numbers that you *should* know as an adult. I know that may not sound like a walk in the park, but trust me, it is *critical* that you read this section. **I strongly believe you've got to know these numbers if you want to get a financial plan that truly works.** The basic information that you're gathering—like your net worth, your monthly take-home income, and your credit score—is what we'll need to start putting together your personalized 50/20/30 program. In fact, this is exactly the info that LearnVest Program clients gather when they start working with a Certified Financial Planner™. Remember that if you have any trouble, you can make a note of your questions at the end of this section. Don't worry, getting your numbers in order won't take longer than a typical spin class and won't make you nearly as tired.

Talk to an **LV** *Expert*

Get Connected

Part of what makes dealing with money complicated for most people is that your financial life exists in a bunch of different places. Your checking account is in one place, your 401(k) is in another, your 529 plan is in yet another—not to mention the receipts lying around your house and in the bottom of your bag. At LearnVest, we created the Money Center to help you get a true snapshot of your money, all in one place. It's free to use, takes approximately two minutes to set up, and will help you answer the following questions faster than ever.

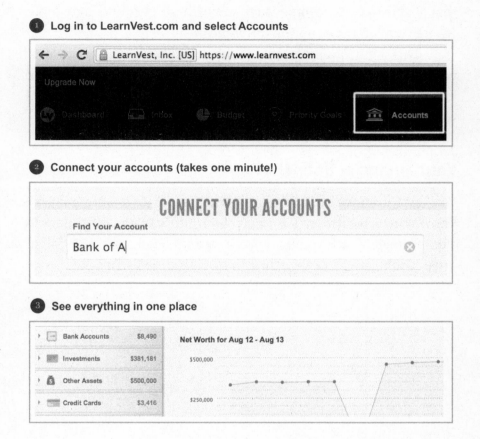

① Log in to LearnVest.com and select Accounts

② Connect your accounts (takes one minute!)

③ See everything in one place

Take a Daily Money Minute

In addition to the added benefit of keeping all your finances organized and in one place, using a tool like LearnVest's Money Center allows you to do a simple yet incredibly powerful exercise: a daily Money Minute. It's how I start each and every day (with a cup of coffee and my laptop or with my iPhone), and I recommend you do the same.

So what is it? Simply start each day by logging on to your

Money Center for one minute—literally. Set a daily calendar reminder until it becomes second nature! Look at every transaction, make sure the charges seem accurate, then look at the folder totals—are you on budget for the month? If not, don't panic; we're all going to have moments when we go over budget. Just know that you'll have to compensate somewhere else and figure out where you can make up the difference.

This kind of awareness about your spending is critical to your overall financial well-being. You know your budget, you know what you care about spending on, and now you'll know if you're staying true to both.

Your Financial Snapshot

You can't improve your financial situation tomorrow if you don't know where your money is today. So right now, I want you to do a quick inventory. If you know your current balances to the dollar, great, you're ahead of the game. If not, it's time to find out.

Your Income

To see what you'll be working with, let's start by figuring out what money is coming in. (If you're a freelancer, just estimate based on last year.)

What is your salary (pretax) this year? $

Will you get any additional income
(say, from a bonus or side job)? $

What is the posttax dollar amount that hits
your bank account as income each month? $

If applicable, what is your partner's salary? $

Will your partner get any additional income? $

What is the posttax dollar amount that your
partner receives as income each month? $

Add up your monthly take-home, your spouse's
monthly take-home (if applicable), plus any
additional monthly income and write it here. $

This is the number you'll be working with when you sit down to plan your 50/20/30 budget.

FEARLESS LESSON   *What Is Your Hour Worth?*

You know what they say. Time is money. But do you know what your time is *really* worth? Say you've been asked to pick up some extra work at $30 per hour. You *could* do it, but you aren't sure it's worth your time. If you are making $100,000 a year, it's probably not, but if you're making $15,000, jump on that freelance! To figure out the price of your hour, just use this simple equation.

Your monthly take-home pay: $_____

Number of days worked in a month: _____ x hours worked per day: _____ = _____ hours worked in a month

Take-home pay/hours worked in a month = $_____ hourly rate

This number sheds light on a common financial mistake that many of us are guilty of—myself included. We spend valuable time to save a few bucks (like traveling forty-five minutes to return a $10 T-shirt), when we could instead put that time toward things that would earn us significantly more in the long run. Other examples: You drive an extra twenty minutes each way to the grocery store to save $5 on dinner. Or you spend an hour on the phone to dispute an $8 credit-card charge. Sure, you saved a few bucks, but the time you spent doing it was worth significantly more. Your time net worth, so to speak, just plummeted.

You have much smarter ways to invest your time. Spend it working toward a raise or bigger bonus. Or toward making sure you're properly insured, so you are never, ever, bankrupted by financial catastrophe. Or researching your investments and reallocating your portfolio. Are these uses of time more challenging? Absolutely. But living your richest life is about big wins. **Make the time, and spend it wisely.**

Your Credit Score

While we're talking numbers, make no mistake: few are as important as your credit score, sometimes called a FICO (Fair Isaac Corporation) score. Your credit score is that all-important number between 300 and 850 that lenders look at to determine how financially responsible you are, and it can play a role in *everything* from what APR (annual percentage rate, aka interest rate) your credit cards have to whether or not you'll be approved for that apartment lease or for the mortgage on your horizon. **I often say**

that your credit score is the only grade that matters once you get out of school, as it is used as the primary measure of your financial reliability.

Not sure what your credit score is? To find out for free, go to CreditKarma.com. For a full free credit *report* (which details exactly why you got the score you did), go to AnnualCreditReport .com. You're entitled to one free report each year from each of the three major credit bureaus: Equifax, Experian, and TransUnion. If you haven't checked them for a while, I recommend combing through all three at once to look for any errors, like debt that's not yours. It might sound like I'm being paranoid, but trust me—it happens! Follow the instructions on the bureau in question for reporting errors. And from now on, request one report from a different credit bureau every four months to stay as up to date as possible. (Put that reminder on your calendar!)

And while you're at it, find out your spouse's or partner's credit score, too, so there are no surprises if you ever apply for a joint loan or mortgage.

What is your credit score? (Example: 760)

If applicable, what is your partner's credit score? (Example: 740)

FEARLESS LESSON   *Monitor for Free*

Contrary to what the Internet may suggest, you don't need to pay for a credit monitoring service or for your credit report. I've found that credit monitoring services are a waste of $10 to $15 a month. Keeping an eye on your credit score and your report (which the government makes available to you for free annually) is enough. If you are paying for a credit monitoring service and get rid of it now, BOOM, there's over $120 more to put into your retirement savings this year.

What the Heck Goes into Your Credit Score

Whether you're thrilled with your score but wondering how you did it or looking to increase one that's lower than you expected, it pays to know exactly what goes into those three mysterious little numbers. Here's a rundown:

FACTOR	ITS IMPACT	SIGNIFICANCE
Payment history	35%	Missing payments hurts your score more than any other factor in this chart.
Credit utilization rate	30%	Your credit utilization rate shows what percentage of your available credit you are using. If it's high, it suggests you may be desperate for credit or financially unstable, since you are spending a lot of money you don't have. On the other hand, if your credit utilization rate is 0%, it could mean that you have poor credit and cannot get a credit card. It's best to be using less than 30%, because it shows that you know how to use credit wisely. For example, if your credit card has a limit of $10,000, aim to charge no more than $3,000 at any given time.
Length of history	15%	This shows how long your accounts have been open and how long it's been since there has been activity in them.
Amount of new credit you have	10%	This tallies what percentage of your accounts have been opened recently and how many recent inquiries were made on your account.
How many types of credit you have	10%	It is better to have varied types of credit, such as credit cards and student loans.

The two most important tips I suggest are:

1. *Never ever* miss a bill and pay your bills in full each month.

2. Be sure to stay under a 30 percent utilization rate of all available debt. This means staying under 30 percent of the credit limit on each credit card. (Better yet: just don't carry any debt.)

FEARLESS LESSON *The High Lifetime Cost of Having a Bad Score*

In her book *Your Credit Score*, Liz Weston considers the fates of two women who are alike in almost every respect: both have student-loan debt, carry a credit-card balance, buy their home, and buy a car. The only difference is that one of them manages credit well and has a 750 credit score and the other manages her credit badly and has a score of 650. The result is that the one with the lower score spends **$200,000(!)** more over the course of her life. If she'd invested that money instead, she could have retired with an **extra $2 million!**[1]

How to Improve Your Credit Score

Since we're on the topic of credit cards, let's talk about some ways to improve your credit score. Having a credit score in tip-top shape will help show future lenders that you're responsible and will help you secure the best interest rates on any debt you need to take out in the future.

Tip 1   **Unload debt.** Maxing out your credit lines hurts your score. Want to avoid that? Only charge what you can afford to pay off right away and never carry debt from month to month.

Tip 2   **Pay all your bills on time, every month.** One late payment can drop your score more than twenty plus points! I recommend setting up calendar alerts so you are always, always, always on time.

Tip 3   **Monitor and fix errors on your report.** Remember that you're entitled to a free credit report every year from each of the three credit bureaus. Space these out every four months, so you can keep an eagle eye on your credit. If there are any red flags, contact the credit bureau ASAP to have them taken care of.

Tip 4   **Pay your parking tickets!** (Did you know those can get turned over to collections agencies, tanking your score?)

Tip 5   **Be mindful about closing accounts.** We recommend you close no more than one bank account a year, and you should never close your oldest account. The length of your credit history plays a big role in your score, so canceling your oldest cards is also a big no-no. And canceling multiple cards cuts down on your available credit, which can ding you as well.

Your Debt

Now we're going to talk about that scary word: debt. If you have debt, know that you are far from alone. According to Federal Reserve statistics, as of December 2012, U.S. consumers held $849.8 billion in credit-card debt. That's $7,117 per household, or $15,257 per indebted household![2]

But did you know that not all debt is bad? We differentiate between what we call good debt and bad debt: Bad debt is debt that doesn't help you make more money later but instead puts you further in the hole (like credit-card debt or payday loans). Good debt, on the other hand, is a means to an end—an investment in your future.

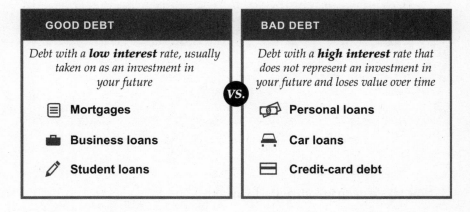

GOOD DEBT		BAD DEBT
*Debt with a **low interest** rate, usually taken on as an investment in your future*	**VS.**	*Debt with a **high interest** rate that does not represent an investment in your future and loses value over time*
Mortgages		Personal loans
Business loans		Car loans
Student loans		Credit-card debt

Tackling debt can feel overwhelming, but that's where I come in. I'm going to walk you through everything you need to know to get rid of that debt in the chapter "The 20." But first you need to take an honest look at the debt you have. So take a few minutes to take stock, then write it all down in one place. Types of debt include credit card, personal loan, car payment, student loans, and unpaid medical bills.

DEBT					
TYPE (credit card, personal loan, car loan, student loan, unpaid medical bills)	BALANCE (what you owe)	MINIMUM MONTHLY PAYMENT DUE (what you're supposed to pay)	ACTUAL MONTHLY PAYMENT (what you pay)	INTEREST RATE	PRIMARY HOLDER (whose name the debt is in)
MasterCard	$5,000	$100	$300	13.99%	Me

Now take a deep breath and add up all your balances. It's okay, don't be scared to look. What is your total debt? $

If this number looks high, don't panic. We're going to get you back on track!

Your Assets

Now let's move on to a much more fun topic: what you *have*. So go pull up all your accounts, including checking, savings, certificates of deposit (CDs), money-market funds, and your emergency fund (if you don't have one yet, don't worry, we'll take care of that in the chapter "The 20"). Your assets should also include retirement savings, including any 401(k), IRA, Roth IRA, or 403(b)s (we'll also run through all this in "The 20"). And don't forget any retirement accounts from previous employers—those still count! If you can't remember whether you have any or where they are, contact the benefits department at your previous job(s).

Fill out these charts to get your assets in order. Don't forget: your noncash assets (real estate, jewelry, art, etc.) count, too!

ASSETS				
TYPE	BANK	BALANCE	CURRENT MONTHLY CONTRIBUTION	IS THIS FOR A SPECIFIC GOAL?
Savings	*HSBC*	*$2,450*	*$50*	*Yes, an emergency fund*

RETIREMENT

TYPE (401[k], Roth 401[k], Roth IRA, Traditional IRA, 403[b], Defined Benefit Plan, Money Purchase Plan, SEP-IRA, TSP, 457 Plan, Pension, Simple IRA)	PRIMARY HOLDER	DOES YOUR EMPLOYER MATCH?	WHAT PERCENT IS MATCHED?	CURRENT BALANCE	HOW OFTEN DO YOU CONTRIBUTE?
IRA	Chase	No	0%	$24,543	$100 monthly, automated

While most people know that they need significant savings to retire on, many workers report having little to no savings. According to the Employee Benefit Research Institute, 60 percent of workers say that the total value of their household's savings and investments is less than $25,000.[3] So if you're feeling a little bummed about the size of your nest egg, take heart. Some savings are better than none!

Net Worth

Now that you know how much you have, we need to do just one more simple step to figure out your net worth. Your net worth is simply your assets minus your liabilities (or debts). To calculate yours, subtract your debts from your assets (using the numbers you wrote in above). What do you get? This is your net worth.

ASSETS − LIABILITIES = NET WORTH

YOUR NET WORTH: $

Is it a number you're feeling pretty good about? If so, congratulations! Is it a negative number? Don't worry. We're going to whip that number into shape together. As long as it starts going up, you're headed in the right direction.

FEARLESS LESSON   *What's in Your Wallet?*

On a daily normal basis I recommend that you carry no more than $100 to $200 and two credit cards. If you lose your wallet (which we are annoyingly likely to do at least a couple of times in the course of our lives, so don't feel bad if it happens to you!), you'll want to have some cash and a credit card at home to tide you over until you can replace everything. Don't carry receipts around, because there's a lot of identifying information on there. Don't carry gift cards unless you're using them right then, because they are the same as cash and can't be replaced if lost. And most important, do not carry your Social Security number around. Now something to add: a cute picture. **Crazy but true: studies have shown that if you include a baby or puppy photo, you have a much higher chance of your wallet being returned if someone finds it!**[4]

Phew! You've just done a lot. And now that we've got that groundwork out of the way, it's time to get to the fun part of this whole financial planning process (seriously!): creating your own personalized 50/20/30 budget. First let's look at what you've accomplished.

What You've Accomplished

- ✓ Calculated your posttax monthly income
- ✓ Determined what your hour is worth at your current salary
- ✓ Checked your credit score
- ✓ Reviewed your credit reports from each bureau for free
- ✓ Set calendar reminders to review one credit report every four months
- ✓ Calculated what you owe in both good and bad debt
- ✓ Calculated your assets (including retirement)
- ✓ Figured out your net worth
- ✓ Learned what exactly to keep in your wallet

Questions for Your Expert

If you still have questions about anything we've covered in this section, write them here and then go to www.learnvest.com/financiallyfearless for answers.

I still don't understand . . .

_____

_____

Where do I find . . .

_____

_____

Talk to an

Lv

Expert

What should I do about my . . .

_____

_____

Examples:

I still don't understand how much my employer matches in my 401(k).

There's an outstanding payment on my credit report that I'm not 100 percent sure is accurate. How do I figure this out?

Summary

Annual salary (before any deductions): $ _____

Monthly take-home income (your salary minus taxes and other deductions): $ _____

Your hour's worth: $ _____

Credit score: _____

Good debt (student loans, investment in your business, mortgage): $ _____

Bad debt (car loans, credit-card debt): $ _____

Total assets (including checking, savings, retirement funds): $ _____

Net worth: $ _____

your
50/20/30
PROGRAM

Now it's time to get to work on your budget. But it's the best kind of work: work you can do in a single evening at home, with a bowl of popcorn by your side and bad TV on in the background.

Listen up: I'm about to tell you a budget tip that changed my life. *Yeah, yeah,* you're probably thinking, *she's about to tell me to skip Starbucks or pack my lunch.* Nope, I wouldn't waste your time with obvious tips like those. We're thinking a little more broadly here. The life changer is a simple ratio dictating how much of your income to allocate for each area of your life. Here's the magical budgeting formula: 50/20/30.

the
50/20/30
rule

50% ESSENTIALS

20% FUTURE

30% LIFESTYLE

Rent/mortgage
Transportation
Groceries
Utilities

Emergency savings
Retirement
Debt repayment
Savings for a home

Restaurants
Shopping
Entertainment
Personal care

FEARLESS LESSON   *How to Nail a Great Budget*

1. **THINK** about the big picture. (What are you trying to accomplish?)

2. **INPUT** your actual numbers. (What do you have to work with?)

3. **LAYER** on the 50/20/30 framework. (Are you already on track or do you need to adjust?)

4. **REFINE** over three months. (Change takes time.)

5. **MONITOR** your progress with a daily Money Minute on LearnVest .com.

Honestly, this 50/20/30 method (touted by Senator Elizabeth Warren, among others) is one of the best things I've ever learned.[1] When I discovered it in the course of my research for LearnVest, I had a true "aha" moment. Why? Because it has *balance built into it.* One of the biggest budgeting traps so many people fall into is focusing on really nitpicky items without seeing the whole picture. We're going to break this mold by thinking **macro.** Our goal here is to see what you're spending where and how making some small changes to your spending pie chart could revolutionize your whole money deal.

Yes, improving the little things—saving a dollar on the cheaper yogurt, skipping our afternoon latte, or walking a mile instead of taking a cab—can make us *feel* like we're in control of our money, but **often we're missing the forest for the trees.** The forest in this case is the big-picture stuff, like the fact that we don't have life insurance, we're massively overspending on our rent, or we're not contributing enough to our retirement.

It's *easier* to focus on clipping a coupon, because we know how to do that and it takes five minutes. Yet it's the things we don't know how to do that are harder but make the *huge* difference and will save us more than even a thousand cheaper yogurts. That doesn't mean you *shouldn't* save on your cab rides or your lunch, but you need to realize that that's just the tip of a pretty substantial iceberg. Better to spend your time blowtorching away said iceberg than chiseling away at the tip with a nail file.

Remember, 50/20/30 represents the percentages of your take-home income that should go to three things: essentials, future, and lifestyle. **50 percent** of your income should go to essential things (we'll discuss what these are in a second). **20 percent** should go to the future, like paying off debt, building an emergency fund, or saving for retirement. And a whopping **30 percent** is yours to play with! You can do whatever the hell you want with it. You can spend it on frog figurines or kung fu DVDs or whatever floats your boat. You could even flush it away if you'd like (though your plumber and I may come over and yell at you).

FEARLESS LESSON   *Why Budgeting Matters*

Did you know that more than half of Americans don't have a basic budget, and 22 percent say they don't have a clear picture of what they spend on housing, food, and entertainment? Not to mention that more than two thirds of Americans say they live paycheck to paycheck.[2] That means that at the end of the month, more than six of every ten people in the country are struggling to pay their bills. Without a budget, your financial picture is at best muddy. At worst you might find yourself overspending, racking up credit-card debt, and feeling confused and anxious about your situation. But a good budget gives you a clear picture of your financial situation so you can live within your means. It will also show you how much you can afford to spend—right down to the dollar—on everything from food ($100? $1,000?) to rent ($500? $5,000?) to travel ($200? $2,000?). And a budget will keep you motivated and accountable toward attaining your financial goals. You wouldn't walk into a busy street with your eyes closed, so why would you *ever* do that with your budget?

Important Note Before You Dive In

50/20/30 is a guiding principle that works for *most* budgets—but we know that money isn't one size fits all. So before you dive in, recognize that your personal budget may need some wiggle room at times. For example, if you're playing catch-up with your retirement savings, your 20 may expand. Or if you're stuck in a lease for an expensive home, your 50 may not be there yet. The goal here is for you to understand what goes into each of these budget categories—your essentials, your future, and your lifestyle—and to understand what a balanced budget *should* look like.

the

—

YOUR ESSENTIALS

Time to dive into the 50 category, the biggest piece of your budget's pie—the essentials. What do I mean by essentials? The first thing you might notice is that most things we may call "essential" in our lives (like an annual beach vacay) are *not* included here. Because our big goal is finding balance in your spending, your *actual* essentials simply include the critical things you need to live and earn your living: shelter (your home, i.e., rent or mortgage), food (groceries, not dinners out), utilities (heat, water, electricity), and transportation to and from work. That's it. We're sticking to the most basic of basics, people.

You may be wondering why 50 percent of your total take-home pay is the magic number here. Here's why: Our ultimate job is to protect you from nasty curveballs. Keeping your essentials to half your budget will give you a cushion. If you max out your budget on all the things you need to survive, what happens when things go awry? If you buy a house out of your price range and 70 percent of your take-home pay goes toward your mortgage, for example, you'll find yourself in a *disaster zone* if you take a pay cut or wind up in the hospital.

Yes, you should *also* have an emergency fund for such code-red events (which I'll explain in the next chapter), but sticking to the 50 percent rule gives you some built-in extra protection and makes space for you to have enough to cover your day-to-day life. Also think about this from the perspective of a dual-income couple. If one partner were to lose his or her job and the couple's income were halved, it would be much easier to still eke by.

So right now, take your monthly income (after taxes, of course), and halve it. If you have a regular salary, you should know this number right away, and if you're a freelancer, ballpark it.

Monthly take-home pay: $

Divided by 2 = $

That's your essentials budget.

For example: You make $75,000 per year. After taxes you make approximately $4,000 per month. Cut that in half, and you get $2,000 to put toward your essentials.

That's the **maximum** I recommend you spend each month on the essentials. No ifs, ands, or buts!

Now let's take a closer look at what makes up your 50 percent.

A Roof over Your Head: Rent or Mortgage

(About 30 Percent)

No matter how good a deal you got on your rent or on your home, this expense is still likely the biggest part of your essentials. I see people overspend here over and over and over again, so let me take a moment to set things straight. **Your rent or monthly mortgage payments should be less than 30 percent of your total take-home salary** (not including any potential bonuses!). Sorry, this is not an ugly rumor or an urban myth. If you've heard this rule before, there's a reason for it: finance experts are nearly unanimous on this.[1]

Let's figure out how much you're currently spending on your rent or mortgage. To make these housing costs as accurate as possible, your total rent calculation should also include anything you pay per month in renter's insurance, and your total mortgage calculation should be your "PITI" (a shorthand way of saying your principal + interest + taxes + homeowner's insurance).

Write your monthly rent or mortgage expenses (PITI) here:
$

Now refer back to your monthly income (see page 55 for a refresher) so we can calculate what percentage your home is eating up:

$$\frac{\textbf{monthly rent/mortgage}}{\textbf{monthly take-home pay}} \times 100 = \textbf{\% of your budget dedicated to your home}$$

Voilà! What percentage are you looking at? Remember that a good benchmark for this number is about 30 percent. That said, I recognize that housing costs vary dramatically from place to place. If you live in an expensive urban center like New York or San Francisco, your rent or mortgage payments may be costlier. **If you fall into this group, recognize that you should still aim to put no more than 50 percent of your overall budget toward essentials,** meaning that you will need to find ways to save on utilities, groceries, or transportation to make up for your higher rent. If your number is higher than 30 percent, don't freak out. I'll get to great tips for lowering these costs momentarily.

Do You Need to Move? (If Not, Move On!)

Okay. You've done the math and you can't afford your current place. Do you just pick up and move? I mean, let's face it, moving is a pain in the ass, and it ain't cheap either. There are brokers' fees and movers' costs (not to mention the costs of replacing the things the movers break) and all the new furniture you'll want to buy once you see how gorgeous the lighting is in your new place. This stuff can add up, even to the point of canceling out what you'll be saving on the rent or mortgage payments.

Plus, even the thought of moving is enough to give me a migraine that no amount of Advil can cure. But hey, getting your financial life in tip-top shape is a lifelong pursuit. You have to start somewhere, and reducing this huge slice of your financial pie by even a little bit can be a good place to start. So let's pause and figure out whether moving to a cheaper place is really worthwhile for *you*.

To Move or Not to Move

If You're a Homeowner

Look, if you have already gone through the major feat of buying a home (and put the thought of all that paperwork behind you), I'm sure the last thing you want to do is stick a FOR SALE sign on your home. That said, if your mortgage payments are extremely painful, it might be something to consider. Here are some questions to ask yourself, as you start to think this through.

1. How much equity do I have in my home?

2. Will the sale result in any capital gains taxes (which kick in after your gains on the sale are more than $250,000 for an individual or $500,000 if you're married)?

Talk to an

LV

Expert

3 If I buy a new house, how much could my monthly payments be?

4 Will my property taxes increase?

Selling a home is a major decision, but take the time to answer these questions and evaluate your living situation more seriously.

If You're a Renter

If you're renting, moving is not quite the headache it would be if you owned. Plus, moving to even a slightly cheaper home or apartment can quickly add up to big savings. You will be doing yourself a huge favor by underpaying on rent. If you broke your lease, the sunk costs wouldn't be easy to stomach, but you might make it worthwhile over just a few months. Here are the questions you can think through.

1 Is my lease almost up, or will I have to break my current lease? If it's the latter, how much will that cost? Will I lose my security deposit? Will I have to find a replacement tenant?

2 What will I have to pay up front to move in (probably first and last months' rent)? Do you have this saved up already? Credit-card debt is not a solution here.

3 How much will it cost to move my stuff? Are we talking a couple of pizzas and some beer for my friends or hundreds of dollars for movers?

4 Will there be space in the new place I'm not using? Can I rent out the extra space?

5 What impact will the new location have on my everyday transportation costs? If the new place is

cheaper, that often means it's less convenient to an urban center. Will I need to buy a car?

Using your best estimate, tally the costs I mentioned above (if applicable):

Cost of breaking a lease: $
Example: One month's rent—$2,000

Up-front costs to move in: $
Example: Security deposit—$1,700

Cost of movers: $
Example: $750

Savings from roommate or renter: $
Example: N/A

**Additional transportation costs (if
transportation is going to get cheaper,
this will be a negative number):** $
*Example: Shorter drive to work so you can save on gas—
−$1,200 per year*

Total: $
Example: $3,250

**If you moved, how much would you save
on rent payments in a year?** $
Example: Old rent = $2,000. New rent = $1,700. Savings = $3,600

**Now just for fun, calculate how much
you'll save in five years:** $
Example: $300 per month for five years = $18,000

FEARLESS TIPS   *If You Make the Move*

If you decide that moving is (or should be) in your immediate future, you still need to decide where, exactly, to move. Keep these two tips in mind to make the whole "underpaying" thing work for you.

Tip 1   BE A PIONEER. Consider moving to the almost-but-not-quite-yet-hip neighborhood. There are a ton of factors that go into choosing a location: proximity to work, how safe you feel in the neighborhood (critical), wanting to live near friends and family, and so on. But if location is something you're flexible on, think about living somewhere off the beaten path. How to recognize the next up-and-coming spot before anyone else does? Find the place where cool stores or restaurants are just starting to crop up. Having a trendy address might be nice, but if the math doesn't work, it doesn't make the cut.

Tip 2   OPT FOR SMALLER TO SAVE BIGGER *EVERYWHERE*. If you've recognized that your housing costs are too high, could you spend less on something slightly smaller—and be just as well sheltered? Once you've lived in a shoebox apartment in Manhattan (as I have), you'll realize you don't actually need as much space as you thought you did. If you had to cut your current place in half, could you still live in reasonable comfort? If so, you're probably looking at halving your home costs. And that's major.

You can go smaller by, well, finding a smaller place (duh), or you could try a more creative solution: get a loft bed or put up a wall to turn a studio into a one-bedroom, and get a roommate; if you're in the burbs, look into renting a guesthouse or a two-family house or duplex.

MONEY MIC: *Why I'm Staying Put*

I've lived in the same four-room apartment for the past seven years, even as my income has risen and fallen and other friends of mine have bought houses or moved on up to bigger places. My husband and I have stayed in this five-hundred-square-foot place (even after having a child) because it's right by our son's public school and I'd rather free up the money I would otherwise be spending on rent for the things I care more about, like my emergency savings fund, my book collection, and my son's after-school classes. By refusing to move to a bigger place, I estimate I've saved $70,000 since my son was born! —Ada, 36, Brooklyn, NY

Bottom line: Your home *is* a choice, and it's up to you to make one that fits your needs, your wants, and your wallet. I promise that getting this expense right will make your life feel richer everywhere else. Wouldn't it be nice to truly enjoy coming home every day to a place that you know makes financial sense for you?

How to Negotiate Your Rent

Not everyone realizes this, but rent is something you can and always should negotiate. In general, you'll have extra leverage if you keep the place in good shape, pay on time, and are a great renter. You're also in a better position if there are a lot of empty homes in the area. Before going into the negotiation, arm yourself with research. Specifically, check sites like Zillow and Trulia (as well as StreetEasy, if you're in the NYC or DC area) to find out what the market looks like. Pay particular attention to comparable prices in your neighborhood. If yours is the only one-bedroom on your block that's so expensive, that's a great chip to use when bargaining with your landlord.

Here are a few others: Can you put some home improvement into the place instead of paying more? That way you'll increase value for the landlord and enjoy the benefits of a fresh coat of paint or a new stove. If the landlord won't budge on price, and moving doesn't make sense for you, can you extend the lease for two years instead of one at that same rate, so you don't have to worry about another hike a year from now? No matter what, be sure to keep reminding him or her what a great and responsible tenant you are. Hey, the worst your landlord can say is no. Give negotiating a shot.

What If You Own?

If you own your own place, your regular monthly mortgage payments come out of this 50 for essentials, just like rent. Since owning a home is also an investment for the future, we'll talk more about the ins and outs of mortgages and how to find the one that's affordable for you in the chapter "The 20." If more than 30 percent of your take-home pay is currently going to those monthly payments, you'll need to find other areas in your budget to make up for this—and potentially consider downsizing in the future.

In the meantime, if you can't reduce your payments, at least you can reduce the pain of making them.

FEARLESS TIPS   *How to Pain-Proof Your Payments*

Tip 1   Making mortgage payments every two weeks instead of every month is a great way to accelerate your pay-down, even if each biweekly payment is half of what you'd otherwise pay monthly. Why does this matter? Because over the course of the year, you end up making the equivalent of **thirteen monthly payments** instead of twelve! This trick helps you pay off your principal in fewer years, which ultimately means not only are you getting free of that debt faster, but you'll also pay less in total interest.

Tip 2   Having a hard time making your homeowner's insurance payment annually? Ask your mortgage company if you can "impound" your mortgage, which means they will escrow the funds along with your mortgage payment. This automates your payment so you never miss it and it doesn't catch you unaware when it comes due.

You Can't Surf the Web by Candlelight:

Utilities (Less Than 5 Percent)

Heat, water, electricity. I know, I know. Snore. But listen. The lesson here is this: **Spend as little as humanly possible on things that aren't fun,** so that you can free up your money for stuff you can actually *enjoy*, like trips, meals, and splurges.

So let's get this over with and see what you can do to reduce those boring utility costs. Note: this does *not* include cable/Internet—though it may not feel that way, cable and Internet are not actually essential to sustain human life. Since heating and electricity costs fluctuate wildly depending on the season (unless you live in L.A., where it's the same season all year), to get the most accurate estimate of how much you're currently spending on utilities, get bills from a variety of months and average them. If you manage these bills online, you should easily be able to flip through past statements and take an average. If you're a paper bills kind of person but don't have the whole year's bills on hand, just do your best to find a typical month's bill and use that number as an estimate.

Write your average monthly utilities expense here: $

Now figure out what percentage of your budget for essentials this consumes:

$$\frac{\text{monthly utilities bill}}{\text{monthly take-home pay}} \times 100 = \% \text{ of your budget dedicated to utilities}$$

There's no exact formula for how much your utilities should cost you, but ideally they should be no more than 3 to 5 percent of your overall budget. Remember that you're building up small pieces of the pie. You wouldn't want something as "blah" as utilities to put you over the top, right?

So how do you get your electric bill down? The average U.S. household spends $2,000 per year just on electricity.[2] But what most people don't realize is how much of it is going to household vampires: appliances, chargers, and devices that suck up energy when they are plugged into the wall, even when they aren't being used. The Energy Information Institute estimates that **10 percent of your electric bill pays for power you aren't using;** and that percentage could be higher if you often leave that laptop in standby mode.[3] Here are some tips for avoiding all those wasted costs.

FEARLESS TIPS   *Electricity and Heat*

Tip 1   Turn off TVs, printers, and computers at night. Want to make this extra easy? Buy a few power strips ($7 each) for the clusters of cords you have near the TV, stereo, and home computer. Then you can gather all those cords in one place so you can simply flip off the switch and be done with it.

Tip 2   Set your fridge's temperature to forty degrees Fahrenheit and your freezer's to zero—any lower and you're wasting energy. Raising your fridge's temperature by just two degrees will save you about $20 per year.[4] How's that for easy savings? All it takes is turning a knob once!

Tip 3   In the winter, turn down your thermostat to sixty-eight degrees. For each degree you lower it, you'll generally save up to 5 percent on your heating bill.[5] Going just from seventy-two degrees to sixty-eight means a potential savings of 20 percent.

Tip 4   There's one more temperature to reduce: your water heater's. Lower it to the recommended temp of 120 degrees. If it was previously set to 140 degrees, studies show you'll save almost $100 per year.[6]

Utility bills are clearly an essential, but they can be difficult to plan for because they're so varied. Say you get used to spending $100 a month on electricity, and then a heat wave hits. Next thing you know, your air conditioner is blasting and you're dealing with a $350 payment. How do you accurately factor in these costs when you can't predict the weather? Most utility companies offer a fixed-budget plan of sorts. They take an estimated average payment due per month (say, $125 in the above example) and allow you to pay that same rate each month. This is a good option if you live in a place with unpredictable weather (which these days we all do) or have ever been caught off guard by a sky-high bill. And not to worry: they'll reconcile this estimated payment with the actual amount due at the end of the quarter or year and offer you credit if you've overpaid. This is a great way to outsmart your utility bill.

Food on the Table: Groceries

(About 10 Percent)

Good news: Your essentials aren't all about mortgage payments and electricity. There's actually some fun stuff hiding in here, like food. You've gotta eat to live! I'm not talking about your "essential" dinner at the best new restaurant in town. I am talking about your basic groceries—the boxes of pasta lining your pantry and the bananas in your fruit bowl. While there's no getting around spending money on food, your groceries must fight for space with utilities and transportation in the last piece of your essentials dough (once home costs are handled), so let's see what we can do to get those costs as low as possible.

All in all, we suggest your groceries should add up to no more than 10 percent of your overall budget. First, let's tally up how much you regularly spend on groceries now. If you connect your accounts to LearnVest's Money Center, you'll be able to see this number in two minutes. If not, pull out your receipts and a calculator.

Write your monthly grocery expenses here: $

Now figure out what percentage of your budget for essentials this consumes:

$$\frac{\textbf{monthly groceries bill}}{\textbf{monthly take-home pay}} \times 100 = \textbf{\% of your budget dedicated to groceries}$$

Is that number more than 10 percent? Don't worry, I've got you covered.

FEARLESS TIPS   *Groceries*

You don't have to be an extreme couponer to save money on groceries. Here are tips even those without scissors of steel should know:

Tip 1   SCOUT DEALS. As someone who doesn't have time to cut coupons, I *do* always grab the coupons in the magazine at the front of the store. It's right there when you walk in, so why not pick it up, skim through it for thirty seconds, and look for anything already on your list? (Having a list alone will help you keep from overspending!) Don't bother ripping or cutting it out—they're just going to scan it when you get to checkout.

Tip 2   SHOP THE PERIMETER. You know how the cookie aisle always seems to just pull you in? Grocery stores are designed so that the fresh foods (produce, dairy, meat, fish, etc.) are stocked along the walls. The inner aisles are filled to the brim with processed foods that are not only bad for you but also overpriced. Stores make 70 percent of their profits from the middle aisles, according to the *Wall Street Journal*.[7] And of course, beware the products near the cash registers, which are there for the sole purpose of inviting you to deviate from your list.[8]

Tip 3 CHECK THE UNIT PRICE. Ten for $20 may sound like a great deal, but you'll usually get the same savings even if you buy only one item. (Let's face it, do you really need ten avocados?) Often this type of offer is just a ploy by the grocery store to get you to buy more than you would otherwise.[9] To see if you're actually getting a good deal, **always check the unit price!**

Tip 4 MAKE BIGGER AND FEWER SHOPPING TRIPS. Many people think it's cheaper to shop daily, buying only what they know they'll definitely eat that day. But it's much better to make one trip a week rather than seven. Shoppers making a "quick trip" to the store usually spend 54 percent more than they planned.[10]

Tip 5 GO GENERIC. Always grab generic brands! I'm going to let you in on a little secret: the products in the flashy wrappers and in the plain ones are almost always exactly the same, minus the marketing budget. Is the OJ carton with the big orange on it really worth an extra $1 compared with the plain white carton?

Tip 6 DON'T OVERSTUFF. Keep your food fresher longer by never overfilling the fridge. And store leftovers in the smallest possible containers that can be tightly sealed.

The Economics of Packing Your Lunch

I'm not going to tell you the obvious here. You know bringing your lunch to work will help you save. But it is worth pointing out *how much*. Let's say that making lunch costs you about $3 per day, while buying costs about $9. Net savings of $6 times four days per week (I'm being realistic here by allowing you at least one day to be lazy or to buy lunch out with coworkers, as building work relationships is an investment in your career) means $1,248 per year. Here's what could happen if you put that into a retirement account: If you're thirty-five now and bring your lunch until your retirement at age sixty-seven and earn 8 percent interest, that's over $200,000, just from brown-bagging your lunches most days.[11] Depending on where you live, that could cover a few years of your retirement. Another bonus? Bringing your lunch tends to keep you skinny!

Getting to Work: Transportation

(About 5 Percent)

How much do you spend on your commute? Take a look first at what you're spending on gas or bike maintenance or a subway card or bus fare. Then think, too, about what kind of time you're losing and what toll that might be taking on your life overall. According to 2009 Census Bureau stats, the average daily commute in the United States is 25.1 minutes, adding up to over sixteen hours per month.[12] That's almost a full day out of your month gone! And our time is valuable.

For your sanity and your budget, you want to get both the cost and the hassle as low as possible, which means taking the time to calculate the true cost of your commute. If the number you get is unbearable, it may be time to move closer to work, switch jobs, or use one of the tips on the next page to streamline your getting-to-work experience.

FEARLESS TIES *Saving on Transportation*

If you use public transportation, check with your employer to see if you can have your monthly costs deducted from your paycheck before taxes. Many companies offer transit checks, which are also pretax. This deduction may save you hundreds per year.

If you drive to work, look into a mileage reimbursement program or think about setting up a carpool.

And that's it for the 50, the essentials. Congratulations, we're halfway to your balanced, personalized budget! Let's look at what you've accomplished.

What You've Accomplished

- ✓ Calculated your 50 (50 percent of your take-home pay)
- ✓ Determined what percentage goes to your home costs
- ✓ Considered whether moving is worth it (if more than 30 percent of your take-home pay is going to your home)
- ✓ Learned how to negotiate your rent
- ✓ Determined what percentage goes to your utilities
- ✓ Considered fixed utility payments (if yours vary dramatically)
- ✓ Adjusted the temperature on your fridge, thermostat, and water heater
- ✓ Determined what percentage goes to your groceries
- ✓ Determined what percentage goes to your transportation
- ✓ Calculated the true time cost of your commute

Questions for Your Expert

If you still have questions about anything we've covered in this section, write them here and then go to www.learnvest.com/financiallyfearless for answers.

I still don't understand . . .

_____

_____

Where do I find . . .

_____

_____

Talk to an

LV

Expert

What should I do about my . . .

_____

_____

Examples:

Where do I find my utility company's payment options?

My commute is an hour each way, but I own my home and the market is down. How do I prioritize?

Summary

Your monthly income (after taxes): $

Half of that (your essentials budget): $

Rent or mortgage: $

Groceries: $

Noncar transportation: $

Car payment: $

Car insurance: $

Gas: $

Maintenance (if you own): $

Renter's/homeowner's insurance: $

Property taxes: $

Electricity: $

Heat: $

Water: $

Total Essentials: $_____, _____ % of overall budget

the

20

—

YOUR FUTURE

Remember that future you fantasized about in the first chapter? This section is where we're going to figure out how to make it a reality.

My dream is to buy a home where my family will grow. I want to be able to pay for my future kids to go to their college of choice, so they can start out their working lives debt free. In the not-so-distant future, I want to take two small vacations each year: one quiet and one adventurous. And when my bones are brittle, I want to have the financial cushion to chill out at the beach and hang with my grandkids.

These are pretty big (read: expensive) dreams. I'm sure your own "wants" in life roll off your tongue just as easily. But how are you supposed to fund all of these things when you're being pulled in so many different directions? Just thinking about all of the priorities we have to juggle when it comes to planning for our financial future—from building emergency savings to funding 401(k) plans to paying off that mortgage so we can own our dream home outright—can make us dizzy. I get how easy it is to feel lost. But this juggling act that we all face boils down to one *huge* question. And it's one of the **biggest, most frequent** questions I encounter all the time:

> **If I have extra money, where should it go first?**

You can imagine that this line of questioning doesn't stop there. It's always followed by a laundry list of choices: Do I pay off my credit-card debt first, or my student loans? Do I save it? Do I invest it? Buy a house? How do I make the smartest decision?

Obviously these kinds of questions all hinge on your personal financial situation, but here's the simple answer that applies to almost anyone: any extra money should be going toward your future.

I told you I'm obsessed with the 50/20/30 method for a reason, and this 20 is it. It's like a hidden gem: a built-in piece of your budget that is meant to get you wherever you want to go. When you commit to putting at least 20 percent of your take-home pay toward your future, you're taking an important step toward life on solid financial ground. Protecting yourself financially means no more tiptoeing along and worrying that a breeze could blow through and totally hurl you off course. No more nights spent tossing and turning, thinking about the safety net you aren't building or the things you won't be able to buy your future children or the future home you won't be able to afford. **The 20 is about reducing and even banishing all these worries.**

Look, I know setting aside 20 percent of your income each month sounds scary, especially if you feel like you're just scraping by as it is, without putting any money into savings. I really do encounter that often. But the cold, hard truth is that if you want to have any hope of someday making your dreams a reality, you'll need to dedicate *at least* 20 percent of your take-home pay to the areas we're going to talk about in this chapter. If you're thinking, *But I just don't have a spare 20 percent to give,* you're wrong. *Everyone,* whether you make $30,000 a year or $300,000 a year, can find ways to save for the future. That's where I come in.

I get that saving is hard. It's all too easy to tell yourself, *I've worked so hard. I deserve to go on a great trip* or *Good-bye, bonus! Hello, new iPad mini!* You *do* work hard. And you do deserve to enjoy each and every day. But I am here to tell you that you deserve . . . *So. Much. More.* You deserve to own your own home outright someday, you deserve to give your children a life full of opportunity, and you deserve to enjoy your golden years.

I'm all for a "carpe diem" mentality, **but not when it comes to your money.** So it's time to shift your thinking, put your 20-plus percent away for your future goals, and then (and *only* then) have fun with whatever is left over. That said, while 20 percent is a good barometer for what you should be doing at a minimum, don't let this percentage limit you if you can actually save more (and reach more goals faster!).

First, What Are You Working With?

I know that planning for the future can be complicated and overwhelming and, in many cases, downright paralyzing. So here's what we're going to do: First, we need to determine how much "extra" *you* have. Then we'll walk through all of the goals you personally need to tackle. If one doesn't apply to you, skip the section!

What is 20 percent of your monthly take-home pay? $

Commit this number to memory. It's what you'll be setting aside *each and every month* for your future priorities.

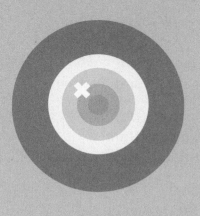

Your Goals

Below I have broken down ten of the biggest and most common goals you may be aiming for. Check the goals that apply to you, writing down any questions you may have along the way for your LearnVest Program expert. Then skip directly to those sections (without passing Go). The most important thing to remember as you read through this section is that no matter what your personal goals are, you *must* put *at least* 20 percent of your total income toward them. How you choose to allocate that 20 percent among them is what you need to figure out. This is not a place to skimp, folks. We're talking about your future here, after all.

☐ Do you need to maximize or start your retirement savings? Note: *Nearly everyone* should be checking this box.
See **Retirement** *on page 103.*

☐ Do you have an emergency fund with at least six months of take-home pay saved up?
If not, see **Freedom Fund** *on page 118.*

☐ Are you carrying any credit-card debt?
If so, see **Credit-Card Debt** *on page 125.*

☐ Are you carrying any student-loan debt, or do you expect to in the future?
If so, see **Student Loans** *on page 144.*

☐ Do you want to buy a home someday?
If so, see **Mortgages** *on page 156.*

☐ Do you plan to have children in the future?
If so, see **Saving for Kids** *on page 169.*

☐ Do you want to save up for your child's education?
If so, see **College Savings** *on page 177.*

☐ Do you have aging parents to help care for?
If so, see **Helping Our Beloved Aging Parents** *on page 185.*

☐ Do you plan to purchase any big-ticket items in the future (car, trip, wedding, etc.)?
If so, see **Major Purchases** *on page 190.*

☐ Do you want to maximize your extra dollars?
If so, see **Other Investments** *on page 193.*

Retirement (Nonnegotiable!)

Think of it this way: You work for approximately forty years to fund seventy-plus years of your life.[1]

Retirement Over Time

Saving	Spending
WORKING (40-PLUS YEARS)	RETIRED

Age 25   Age 67   Age 95

— 70 years —

That's a **whole lot** of time, so if you don't put aside income for those nonworking years now, well, it's not going to be pretty. Saving for retirement is *major* and *everyone* needs money to fall back on in later years. To fully retire in your sixties, you'll need lots of money, so if there's one thing you do immediately as a result of reading this book, it should be saving harder and faster for retirement. **Retirement cannot be neglected,** despite the other financial responsibilities tugging at you.

FEARLESS LESSON   *Maximize Your Dollars*

Let's say you have a spare dollar. How do you best maximize it? Thanks to compounding interest, $1 in your retirement savings will yield exponentially more than $1 in a savings account. If you have it in an account that yields a 6 percent return, in forty years it will be worth $10.[2] That probably does not sound like a lot, but think about the effect on a larger scale: put aside $100,000 for retirement and it could grow to $1 million. While paying down debt and saving for emergencies are smart money moves, too, your retirement dollars can bring some serious value.

Retirement is becoming a growing problem in America. On the plus side, we're living longer, but we're not prepared to handle that financially. The stats on retirement are just crazy: 30 percent of American workers plan to work until they're over eighty years old.[3] If you're anything like me, you'll want to *relax* once you've reached that age. Also, what if you *can't* work at eighty because your body or mind can't swing it? You will have had a whole lifetime of hard work. Why not make sure you can enjoy the payoff?

Retirement savings goals are big. And often, big goalposts can stop you in your tracks. It's nothing to be ashamed of; it's human nature. You may think that an extra 1 percent in monthly 401(k) contributions will hardly make a dent. Or that putting aside $50 a week into an IRA won't really matter. Wrong. So before we actually crunch some numbers, let me just say this: *every little bit helps*. Do what you can. Make progress. You'll get there.

So how much am I talking? Let's get a little more specific on how big a nest egg you should be gunning for. At LearnVest we think of annual retirement needs in terms of replacement value: what percentage of your current income will you need in order to replace not having an income for each year of retirement? This percentage will depend on your personal situation, so once you look at the numbers, you have to ask yourself, "Can I see myself living on *x* number of dollars a year?" During retirement, there are expenses that tend to decrease (for example: perhaps you've paid off your mortgage, student loans, and consumer debt, and no longer financially support your grown children). But there are also some that tend to increase (for example: health care for your aging self and trips around the world). Given these competing factors, we generally estimate that you'll need to replace **at least 70 percent** of your current income to stay above water. We've crunched the numbers to show you what that looks like at a few income levels.

ANNUAL CURRENT SALARY	RETIREMENT SALARY IN TODAY'S DOLLARS (assumes 70% replacement ratio)	RETIREMENT SALARY IN FUTURE DOLLARS (assumes 70% replacement with 3% inflation annually)	TARGET NEST EGG (assumes you'll need your retirement salary for 20 years)
$35,000.00	$24,500.00	$59,467.93	$884,732.64
$50,000.00	$35,000.00	$84,954.19	$1,263,903.77
$65,000.00	$45,500.00	$110,440.44	$1,643,074.91
$80,000.00	$56,000.00	$135,926.70	$2,022,246.04
$100,000.00	$70,000.00	$169,908.37	$2,527,807.55
$125,000.00	$87,500.00	$212,385.47	$3,159,759.43
$150,000.00	$105,000.00	$254,862.56	$3,791,711.32
$200,000.00	$140,000.00	$339,816.75	$5,055,615.10
$300,000.00	$210,000.00	$509,725.12	$7,583,422.64
$500,000.00	$350,000.00	$849,541.86	$12,639,037.74

FEARLESS LESSON *Don't Leave Money on the Table*

If you remember nothing else from this chapter, know this golden rule: *maximize your employer match.* If your employer matches your 401(k) contributions up to, say, 5 percent, **you should be putting away whatever amount it takes to get the full company match.** (If you don't know what the amount is, contact your HR rep ASAP.) It's *free* money!

Not only that, with a dollar-for-dollar match, you're getting a *100 percent* return on your investment. It may hurt a little bit to see the size of your paycheck reduced, but it's a small price to pay for having your employer help fund your life. Failing to maximize this benefit is leaving money on the table. **If your employer doesn't offer matching, this doesn't mean you're off the hook with retirement savings.** On the contrary: this just means it's even more important to contribute as much as possible.

"But I *Can't* Save, Because . . ."

Putting money away for retirement conjures up a whole range of excuses, and believe me, I've heard them all. What are the most common things we tell ourselves to avoid saving for retirement? Oh, where to begin!

> **Excuse 1: I can't afford it.** Nearly one in four people say they don't have money to contribute to retirement after all the bills are paid.[4] It might feel that way sometimes, but if we can find the $50 to go out to dinner every Tuesday night, we *can* find $200 a month to put in a retirement account. Make this happen, even if you have to do it one dollar at a time over the course of the month. And if you think putting away $50 a week won't make a difference, consider this: Contribute just $200 a month for thirty years, and if your money grows on average 8 percent a year, your total contributions of $72,000 will grow to almost $300,000 if put away for thirty years. When you think about it that way, skipping that regular Tuesday dinner doesn't seem so bad, does it?

Excuse 2: I'm young. There's plenty of time to save for retirement later. This is one of the most seductive retirement lies. For a good long while, it is true that retirement is a ways off. (Even if you're fifty-five, it's still at least ten years away.) But the longer you put off saving for retirement, the less interest you'll earn *and* the more difficult it will be for you to save. When I was in college, I saw a graph on compounding interest. Just like this one:

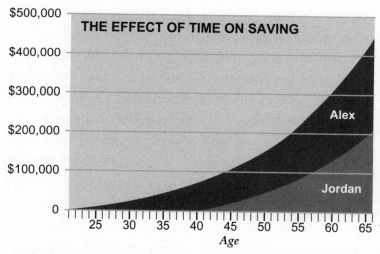

Alex and Jordan both put just over $90,000 in their retirement accounts over the years, but Alex began saving ($2,000 per year) at age twenty-two, while Jordan began saving (about $3,500 per year) twenty years later at age forty-two. Even though they both put in the **same total amount,** Alex will have over twice as much money at retirement as Jordan will when they reach age sixty-seven (assumes a 6% annual rate of return). That's because her money had more time to grow, so it was able to make more off of itself than Jordan's. *Note: This is illustrative and is not reflective of guaranteed profits over time. Actual results may fluctuate based on market conditions.*

It fundamentally changed my view of my money. Seriously, you have two people who put the *same* dollar amount into their retirement funds. The one who started twenty years later contributed the same amount, but ended up with less than half as much.

As someone who cares about making my money work

for me, this visual speaks volumes. It turns out that one of the smartest things you can do is simply to get **time on your side.** This is how you shortcut the hard work—by taking advantage of the power of compounding interest and the fact that you will only have an increasing number of financial obligations pulling at your purse strings as the years go by.

So, this is not something you can keep putting off. This is something to tackle today. The time is now.

Excuse 3: When I get married someday, I won't have to worry about money. I bet all the married people reading this are having a good laugh right now. Marriage does not automatically make your financial life easier. The effect of marriage on your finances depends on a host of factors: Do you both work? Do you both make enough to support yourselves? If one or both of you got laid off, could you still afford your rent or mortgage? Are you honest with each other about your spending? Do you agree on your financial goals? Will you have children? If so, do you make enough that one of you can stay home with them? Bottom line: this is an outrageous excuse, and now I am drinking wine.

Retirement Savings Options for Stay-at-Home Parents

When you're working, your employer will often facilitate your retirement savings by taking money right out of your paycheck and putting it into savings so you don't have to think about it. But what are you supposed to do as a stay-at-home parent?

1. When you leave the workforce, roll over your 401(k) into an IRA.
2. Set up a spousal IRA if you file a joint return with your spouse.
3. Open an individual 401(k) or a SEP-IRA if you're self-employed.
4. Increase your spouse's 401(k) contribution.

Excuse 4: What about Social Security? I'll just live off that when I retire. Maybe *today's* retirees can say this. But the future of Social Security is uncertain. Anyone retiring in the coming years should not rely on this as a be-all and end-all. If the system doesn't go bankrupt and you get to receive Social Security benefits, great. If not, what's your plan B? I don't know about you, but that's a risk I won't take.

Excuse 5: I deserve to have fun with my money *today*—I work hard for it. I hear you. But saving for retirement versus enjoying life now is not an either/or proposition. You *can* do both. Also, let me put it this way: yes, you deserve to enjoy your money now, but you also deserve not to count pennies when you're old and gray.

Excuse 6: An inheritance is coming my way someday. This is a case of counting chickens before they hatch. You never know what could happen to the inheritance (it could be devoured by medical bills, it could dwindle away in a financial crisis, or you may need it to pay off debts or taxes of the estate). Sure, it would be nice to inherit a windfall and be able to put it toward your retirement, but counting on doing so is **not a plan;** it's a gamble at best. It's far safer to plan to fund your own retirement and then enjoy your inheritance as a bonus if you do indeed receive one.

Excuse 7: The market is down, so why bother to invest in a retirement account? Yes, the market is unreliable from year to year, and yes, the value of your investments will dip in a down market. But downswings don't last forever, and historically, over long periods of time, the market has shown solid returns. While past performance doesn't reveal future returns, the S&P 500, for example, has averaged 9.28 percent annual returns over the last twenty-five years.[5]

Alternatively, let's say you leave your money under your mattress or even in a savings account bearing 1 percent interest: you're going to lose the purchasing power of those dollars due to inflation (which is estimated at 3 percent).[6] Yes, with the market, you're opening yourself up to some risk—but with risk comes reward.

Excuse 8: I'll start saving when the market improves. No one can predict the market. No one. So while it's true that you cannot time your investments perfectly so that they only ever go up, history has shown that if you invest regularly over decades, your investments should experience more ups than downs. So invest for the long haul, and don't fret over minor dips now. If you do, you'll be missing out on an opportunity to amass money later.

Excuse 9: I'll be able to use the equity in my home to retire. Sure, selling your home will free up lots of cash . . . but then where will you live? And what if the market is down when you want to sell that home? Remember the housing crisis a few years ago? The one where tens of thousands of near retirees were left without nest eggs after the values of their homes plummeted? This is not your smartest game plan.

Excuse 10: I need to get my kids through college first, and then I can focus on my retirement. Yes, college is a big expense, and you should definitely save for it—that is, once your own retirement needs are taken care of. If you're a parent, it's a natural instinct to put your children's futures before your own. But think about it this way: if you don't save the full amount for your children's college education, you can always fall back on financial aid, grants, scholarships, and student loans to help pay your children's way. When it comes to your retirement, however, there are no loans. Let me repeat: there are *no* loans. All you'll have to live on is what you've saved. For that reason, saving for retirement should be your top financial priority—always.

I get that you don't want to saddle your kids or future kids with loans—what parent would? But remember that if you pay for your children's college and then cannot afford your retirement, you will end up burdening your children all the same. They will feel obligated to help you out—at a time when their own families need them financially.

Excuse 11: I plan to keep working even during retirement.
You may love your work, and it may be the kind of work you can even imagine yourself doing well into your seventies or eighties. But while that's easy to say now, what if you can't find work at that point in your life, or what if you have health problems or family obligations that prevent you from working? While there is nothing wrong with *hoping* for a best-case scenario, it isn't wise to plan around one. Sock away some money now so you're ready for whatever may come your way. The last thing I ever want you to deal with is a health issue *and* money concerns at the same time.

Where Should You Keep Your Retirement Savings?

Fortunately, 401(k)s are not the only retirement vehicle out there. Let's start with an overview of the major retirement savings options available.

TYPE OF ACCOUNT	DESCRIPTION	TAXES ON CONTRIBUTIONS?	TAXES ON WITHDRAWALS (PRINCIPAL)?	TAXES ON EARNINGS?
401(k)	An employer-sponsored account into which you can save pretax money from every paycheck. In retirement, the money you withdraw—including earnings—will be taxed in whatever income bracket you're in at the time.	No	Yes	Yes
403(b)	Operates almost exactly like a 401(k) plan but is usually offered to those who work for public schools and tax-exempt organizations.	No	Yes	Yes
Traditional IRA	An individual retirement account into which you can save money and receive a tax deduction if you meet certain income requirements or if you don't have an employer-sponsored retirement plan—such as a 401(k)—available to you.	No	Yes	Yes
Nonde-ductible IRA	An individual retirement account into which you can save money if you don't meet the income requirements for a traditional IRA and you have an employer-sponsored retirement plan available to you. Your contributions to this plan are not deductible on your taxes, but that also means you won't pay taxes on the money when you withdraw it during retirement. You will, however, pay taxes on any earnings.	Yes	No	Yes
Roth IRA	An individual retirement account into which you can save after-tax money if you meet certain income requirements. In retirement, the money you withdraw—both your deposits and all of your earnings—is entirely tax free.	Yes	No	No

Each of these account types is essentially the bucket you'll put your investments in. Not sure which bucket is right for you? Everyone's retirement situation is unique, so this is a moment when a retirement expert can provide extra clarity.

If you want to get a head start, try the handy flow charts on pages 113 and 114.

If your tax-filing status is Single

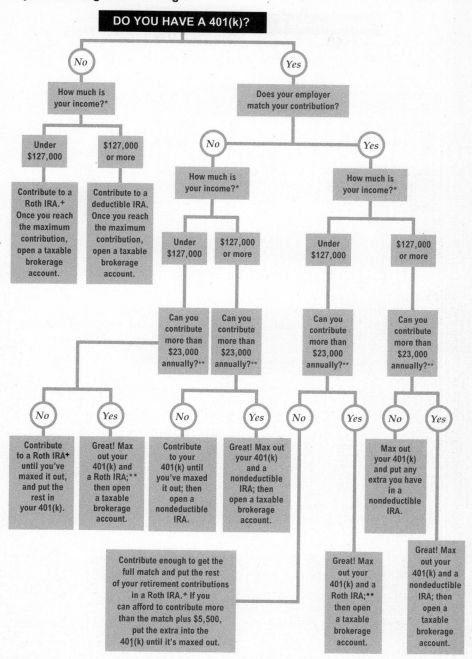

DO YOU HAVE A 401(k)?

No

How much is your income?*

- **Under $127,000** — Contribute to a Roth IRA.+ Once you reach the maximum contribution, open a taxable brokerage account.
- **$127,000 or more** — Contribute to a deductible IRA. Once you reach the maximum contribution, open a taxable brokerage account.

Yes

Does your employer match your contribution?

No

How much is your income?*

- **Under $127,000** — Can you contribute more than $23,000 annually?**
  - **No** — Contribute to a Roth IRA+ until you've maxed it out, and put the rest in your 401(k).
  - **Yes** — Great! Max out your 401(k) and a Roth IRA;** then open a taxable brokerage account.
- **$127,000 or more** — Can you contribute more than $23,000 annually?**
  - **No** — Contribute to your 401(k) until you've maxed it out; then open a nondeductible IRA.
  - **Yes** — Great! Max out your 401(k) and a nondeductible IRA; then open a taxable brokerage account.

Yes

How much is your income?*

- **Under $127,000** — Can you contribute more than $23,000 annually?**
  - **No** — Contribute enough to get the full match and put the rest of your retirement contributions in a Roth IRA.+ If you can afford to contribute more than the match plus $5,500, put the extra into the 401(k) until it's maxed out.
  - **Yes** — Great! Max out your 401(k) and a Roth IRA;** then open a taxable brokerage account.
- **$127,000 or more** — Can you contribute more than $23,000 annually?**
  - **No** — Max out your 401(k) and put any extra you have in a nondeductible IRA.
  - **Yes** — Great! Max out your 401(k) and a nondeductible IRA; then open a taxable brokerage account.

*By income, we mean your modified adjusted gross income. This convoluted name reflects the convoluted way in which it is calculated. First you subtract various items, such as education expenses or IRA contributions, from your income to determine your adjusted gross income (which is used for tax purposes). Then you add back in other items, such as student-loan deductions and foreign income, to get your modified adjusted gross income.

+The rules for eligibility and contribution limits for a Roth IRA change every year. In 2013, if your modified adjusted gross income was less than $112,000, you could contribute the maximum amount, which was $5,500 (or $6,500 if you were fifty or older). If your modified adjusted gross income was between $112,000 and $127,000, you were eligible to make a partial contribution.

**$23,000 is the combined 401(k) and IRA contribution limit, $17,500 and $5,500, respectively (in 2013).

If your tax-filing status is Married Filing Jointly

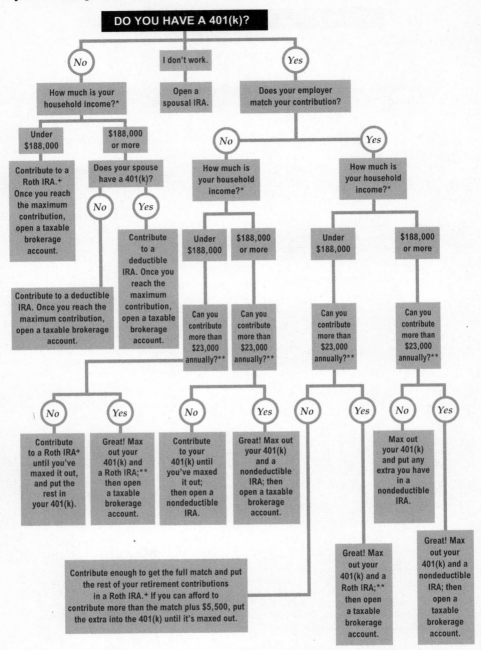

DO YOU HAVE A 401(k)?

No

How much is your household income?*

I don't work.

Open a spousal IRA.

Yes

Does your employer match your contribution?

Under $188,000

$188,000 or more

Contribute to a Roth IRA.+ Once you reach the maximum contribution, open a taxable brokerage account.

Does your spouse have a 401(k)?

No

Yes

Contribute to a deductible IRA. Once you reach the maximum contribution, open a taxable brokerage account.

Contribute to a deductible IRA. Once you reach the maximum contribution, open a taxable brokerage account.

No

How much is your household income?*

Yes

How much is your household income?*

Under $188,000

$188,000 or more

Under $188,000

$188,000 or more

Can you contribute more than $23,000 annually?**

Can you contribute more than $23,000 annually?**

Can you contribute more than $23,000 annually?**

Can you contribute more than $23,000 annually?**

No

Yes

No

Yes

No

Yes

No

Yes

Contribute to a Roth IRA+ until you've maxed it out, and put the rest in your 401(k).

Great! Max out your 401(k) and a Roth IRA; then open a taxable brokerage account.**

Contribute to your 401(k) until you've maxed it out; then open a nondeductible IRA.

Great! Max out your 401(k) and a nondeductible IRA; then open a taxable brokerage account.

Max out your 401(k) and put any extra you have in a nondeductible IRA.

Contribute enough to get the full match and put the rest of your retirement contributions in a Roth IRA.+ If you can afford to contribute more than the match plus $5,500, put the extra into the 401(k) until it's maxed out.

Great! Max out your 401(k) and a Roth IRA; then open a taxable brokerage account.**

Great! Max out your 401(k) and a nondeductible IRA; then open a taxable brokerage account.

*By income, we mean your modified adjusted gross income. This convoluted name reflects the convoluted way in which it is calculated. First you subtract various items, such as education expenses or IRA contributions, from your income to determine your adjusted gross income (which is used for tax purposes). Then you add back in other items, such as student-loan deductions and foreign income, to get your modified adjusted gross income.

+The rules for eligibility and contribution limits for a Roth IRA change every year. In 2013, if your modified adjusted gross income was less than $173,000, you could contribute the maximum amount, which was $5,500 (or $6,300 if you were fifty or older). If your modified adjusted gross income was between $173,000 and $188,000, you were eligible to make a partial contribution.

**$23,000 is the combined 401(k) and IRA contribution limit, $17,500 and $5,500, respectively (in 2013).

FEARLESS TIP *Traditional vs. Roth IRA*

If you have a traditional IRA, consider *converting* your IRA to a Roth. Since there is no income restriction to do this and the investment earnings on a Roth are not going to be taxable if you stick it out until age 59.5, you could reap larger tax rewards. Plan to pay any conversion taxes out of pocket, not out of the account balance.

If do you this, consider how the conversion will affect your income levels (and thus tax bracket) for the year. You may want to do the conversion over a period of years to avoid suddenly jumping into a higher bracket.

Okay, so you get that retirement is urgent, and you've encountered your excuses head on, so you can put them aside. But before we move on to your other major "20" goals, there are two more things you need to know:

FEARLESS LESSON *Investing 101*

To reach your retirement goal, a simple savings account is not going to cut it. You'll need a comprehensive investing strategy. Not only do you want to maximize each and every dollar, but you'll also need to account for inflation, which means that prices on everything (from high chairs to hybrids) go up every year. Left under your mattress, your dollar's spending power will slowly but surely diminish over time. Over the long term, inflation has averaged about 3 percent per year, which means that if you put $1,000 in a shoe box in your closet today and let it sit for forty years, you'll still have $1,000—but it will only be worth about $306 in today's dollars.[7]

Talk to an LV *Expert*

Instead, if you invest that $1,000 and earn 5 percent a year for forty years, you could end up with $7,040, or about $2,158 in today's dollars.[8] Considering that you want to live a long life, you'll need to maximize your dollars for the long run.

FEARLESS LESSON *Never, Ever Take Money out of a Retirement Account*

You will be taxed and penalized like crazy. Get another job, borrow from a family member, and exhaust all other options before you even *think* about withdrawing retirement savings. Enough said.

With all the confusing and complicated options out there, it can be incredibly overwhelming to figure out where we *should* be investing our retirement savings. If you still have questions, this is a perfect time to enlist some professional guidance. **You don't have to go it alone.**

What You've Accomplished

✓ Determined how much you need in retirement (based on your replacement ratio)

✓ Learned the major types of retirement accounts

✓ Gotten any excuses out of the way

✓ Learned how to cover retirement if you're a stay-at-home parent

✓ Realized the importance of a retirement investment strategy

Questions for Your Expert

If you still have questions about anything we've covered in this section, write them here and then go to www.learnvest.com/financiallyfearless for answers.

I still don't understand . . .

_____

_____

Talk to an
LV
Expert

Where do I find . . .

_____

_____

What should I do about my . . .

_____

_____

Examples:

I have a 401(k) from my old job. Do I need to roll it over?

How do I know what kind of retirement accounts I have?

I plan to increase my salary dramatically over the next few years. Do I use my anticipated salary to calculate my retirement needs?

Does my employer match?

Should I roll over my IRA?

Freedom Fund

Throughout this book, you'll hear me talk about your emergency fund *a lot*, and that's because **it's the best way to protect yourself in a true crisis.** I can't tell you what surprises life will throw your way, but I can tell you that they *will* happen and that you need to have the money to get through them financially unscathed. At LearnVest, we believe your emergency fund should contain *at least* **six months' worth** of net income (up to a year is our recommendation if you have kids or other dependents), and you should only touch it in a true emergency (and no, your family vacation to Hawaii is *not* a true emergency). This is a point that bears repeating: unless there is a true emergency, it should sit patiently and liquidly in a savings account, waiting for you should you need it (God forbid).

FEARLESS LESSON   *Freedom Funds Are Not Optional*

I like to call the emergency fund "a freedom fund," because it gives you the freedom to get out of bad situations. If you need to leave a crappy relationship, you have the freedom to pick up and go. If you just can't take another day at your job, you have the freedom to take some time off. If a loved one needs you, you have the freedom to be there for them. Personally, my fund allowed me to leave business school and start LearnVest. It gave me the freedom to launch my dream career.

A study conducted in 2011 by the National Foundation for Credit Counseling revealed that 64 percent of Americans didn't have even $1,000 saved for an emergency![9] Puhleez, don't be one of them!

While an ideal emergency fund is at least six months of net income stored in a savings account, it's best to have upwards of nine months saved if your job is unstable or you work as a freelancer and have an irregular income. Are you in an unstable financial position? If so, aim for nine months to a year.

Calculating Your Emergency Fund

At the minimum, what is your monthly take-home pay x 6? $ _____

Is your job insecure? What is your monthly take-home pay x 9? $ _____

Do you have dependents to support? What is your monthly take-home pay x 12? $ _____

This is how much to aim for in your freedom fund: $ _____

Why a Higher Salary May Mean Bigger Risk

If you make a good salary, you might be tempted to think you don't need this safety net. *Au contraire!* The better educated and the more senior you are in your job, the more savings you should have in your emergency fund so you can ride out any periods without work. Why? **Because the higher up you are, the longer it could take to find a new job on the same career trajectory.**

Similarly, the more specialized your job is, the longer it could take to get back on track after unemployment. Additionally, don't think that if you lose your job, you'll find work any faster just because you have a degree. In fact, as of 2010, 20 percent of the unemployed had college degrees—and that doesn't even include the "underemployed" (those working fewer hours or at a level far below their skill set).[10] If you may be overqualified for a lot of the jobs, make sure you have nine months' worth of your take-home pay in a savings account, just in case.

As I may have mentioned once or twice, the money in this fund is best left untouched unless there is a true emergency. Here are five examples of situations that qualify:

Emergency 1. You've lost your job and need to continue paying rent, bills, and other living expenses.

Emergency 2. You have a medical or dental emergency.

Emergency 3. Your car breaks down and is your primary form of transportation.

Emergency 4. You have emergency home expenses. For example, your A/C breaks down in hundred-plus-degree weather, your roof is leaking, your basement is flooded (and no, a kitchen in need of redecorating doesn't count, no matter how much you hate that wallpaper).

Emergency 5. You have bereavement-related expenses, like travel costs for a family funeral.

Here's another reason why you should always have money in a freedom fund: if you don't, and one of these five types of emergencies arises, you'd likely be stuck using a credit card to handle it, leading you into (or deeper into) credit-card debt. In fact, medical expenses are the **leading** contributor to credit-card debt, with low- to moderate-income households averaging $1,678 in credit-card debt due to out-of-pocket medical expenses.[11]

Plus, paying for emergency expenses on your credit card (if you don't pay off your bill immediately) will end up costing you more over time, as you'll rack up interest payments as you try to dig yourself out of debt. Having a fund will not only save you more money in the long run but also **give you peace of mind in knowing you have the safety net to catch those unexpected curveballs when they arrive.**

How to Grow Your Freedom Fund

If getting six months of take-home pay together seems daunting, here are eight tricks:

1. **Direct deposit into your savings.** This is my personal favorite! Think of *yourself* as a regular monthly bill you have to pay. All you have to do is arrange to have a set amount of money directly deposited from your paycheck into a savings account each month. I recommend using a separate savings account because if you have access to your funds in your checking account, you're more likely to spend them. Again, it might hurt a bit at first to take home a little less every month, but trust me, after a while you won't even notice it's gone. Here's a moment when the "set it and forget it" strategy works wonders.

2. **Never spend a bonus again.** It feels great to be rewarded for your hard work. And it feels even better

to spend that hard-earned bonus on something you'll enjoy, like a trip to France or an iPad. At the same time, the pleasure of a vacation or new gadget is short-lived compared to financial security. So make a pact with yourself to put every bonus you get from here on out to good use. If you direct 90 percent of your bonuses straight into your savings account as a rule, you'll still have 10 percent to treat yourself with (plus the comfort of knowing that you're building a well-earned safety net). **I live by this rule.**

3 **Go nuts cutting your unnecessary costs.** Okay, okay, this seems like an obvious one—and easier said than done. Actually, most people spend money on more unnecessary items than they think. So take time to look at where your money is going in detail and begin to cut back. Saving $10 here and there could help you put a lot away in the long run.

4 **Open a seasonal savings account.** Many banks offer seasonal accounts meant to save for holidays like Christmas. These accounts give you reduced access to your accounts, charging a hefty penalty each time you withdraw more than permitted. Since emergencies don't occur often, a seasonal account could make sure you're touching it only when needed (just make sure you're not tempted to blow it all on Christmas gifts).

5 **Sell unused items.** I love this one. Chalk it up to my massive craving for organization, but I'm all about getting rid of things I no longer use. Rather than throwing these unused goods away, start selling them, and put that money into your emergency fund. All you need to do is post them to a site like eBay or Craigslist or Amazon and you can get rid of items from the

comfort of your home. You can also take your clothes to a consignment shop to have them sold for you.

6 **Stop spending $5 bills.** Instead of saving your pennies, put aside any $5 bills that come your way. Never spend a $5 bill again, and you'll be surprised by how quickly this silly trick will help you come up with a few hundred dollars to add to an emergency fund.

7 **Earn extra income.** You could pick up odd jobs via websites like TaskRabbit.com, DoMyStuff.com, Elance.com, FreelanceSwitch.com, or Sitters.com.

8 **Use "cash back" rewards.** If you get a cash-back reward for any spending on your credit card, just make it a rule that those dollars will be dedicated to your freedom fund. It may only add up to $100 extra each year, depending on your spending, but every little bit counts.

What You've Accomplished

✓ Calculated your freedom-fund goal amount (6, 9, or 12 months)

✓ Learned when you can (and cannot) use your freedom fund

✓ Opened a savings account for this goal (if you didn't have one already)

✓ Set up a direct deposit into your freedom fund account

✓ Put a plan in place to build up this account quickly (from cutting costs to earning extra income on the side)

Questions for Your Expert

If you still have questions about anything we've covered in this section, write them here and then go to www.learnvest.com/financiallyfearless for answers.

I still don't understand . . .

_____

_____

Where do I find . . .

_____

_____

What should I do about my . . .

_____

_____

Examples:

How do I calculate how much my freedom fund should be if I'm a free-lancer and have an inconsistent monthly income to begin with?

How do I know if my bank offers the best savings account for this goal?

Talk to an LV *Expert*

Credit-Card Debt

Remember, we believe there is a difference between good and bad debt. Bad debt is debt you've taken out that is not an investment in your future. It includes credit cards and car loans. Of course, all debt feels absolutely awful. I always joke that there are two things in life that are easy to gain and nearly impossible to lose: weight and credit-card debt. Bad debt in particular is *designed* to grow quickly. It snowballs. It feels out of control. To put it succinctly: it sucks.

Bad debt typically comes with higher interest rates and reaps no returns. The vacation you put on your credit card and the shiny new car you drove off the lot may feel good in the moment, but unlike your home, they are never going to appreciate in value.

There are two critical reasons for making this debt a thing of the past, pronto. First, it's a massive emotional burden. (I could talk for *hours* about this.) If there's one financial issue that keeps people up at night, it's bad debt. Second, it damages your entire financial profile. Carrying a balance on your credit cards can ding your credit score, which means higher interest rates, which means that *in addition to* the mounting debt, you'll be in the position of throwing away hard-earned cash toward interest. Think about what a terrible hamster wheel that is if you're earning money, making credit-card payments, and *not even making a dent in the debt you owe.*

If you are like most Americans and you do have credit-card debt, even a lot of it, do *not* feel bad. It is totally unhelpful to beat yourself up or send yourself down a shame spiral. **You are *far* from alone.** At the time of writing, roughly half of American households have credit-card debt.[12] The good news is that this debt need not hang over your head forever. In this section I'm going to give you the tools to say *sayonara* to bad debt—for good.

If you need some convincing that now is the time to start, take a look at what this example of being $5,000 in debt could mean to your budget.

Revolving Debt

Debt	$5,000
How long?	5 years
Monthly payment	$118.95
APR	15%
Total over time	$7,137
How much extra did you pay?	**$2,137**

Assume it takes you five years to pay off $5,000 of debt, making minimum monthly payments of $118.95, with a 15 percent APR. Once the debt balance is zero, you will have paid $2,137 in interest alone.

Among the things you **could have bought instead:**

- Airfare to Europe for two

- Food, diapers, clothing, and toiletries for a baby's first year of life

- New furniture for a room in your home

- A really nice flat-screen TV

Crazy, right? Okay, let's get rid of that debt once and for all.

How to Get Debt Free

Step 1. Get Inspired

Read this:

MONEY MIC: *How I Paid Off $90,000 of Debt in Just Three Years*

At twenty-six, I was working hard and playing hard. I thought that I had everything under control—despite living practically paycheck to paycheck, having significant credit-card debt, and paying the minimum on my student loans.

Luckily, someone special woke me up to the reality of my financial situation. It took a lot of hard work, but three years later, I'm almost debt free.

I knew from the outset of my college search that my parents had limited funds, but that didn't stop me from attending school out of state—both for my undergraduate degree and my master's. I funded both degrees with student loans. On top of that, I put some of my living expenses on credit cards—so by the time that I got my master's, I had accumulated tens of thousands in student-loan debt and almost $9,000 in credit-card debt.

After graduating, I moved to DC, where I got a job at a non-

profit that paid $50,000 a year—and lived as though I didn't have any debt. I paid the minimum on my loans and spent $1,400 a month for a studio apartment in a hip neighborhood.

Three years ago, I met Rob. One night six months into our relationship, I told him about my (ballpark) debt. It wasn't exactly a deal breaker, but he didn't take it well. This was a guy who was in a great financial situation. At twenty-six, he was already saving for a house!

That night I went home and plugged all of my debt into a spreadsheet. It was a smack in the stomach: I owed almost $90,000. At the rate I was going, it would take me 112 months to pay off my debt—and that didn't include interest. To tackle all of my debt, I started by making a budget. I also calculated my monthly expenses and tried to determine what it would take to put $500 to $1,000 extra each month toward putting a further dent in my loans. I got creative: I gave up my studio and found a roommate in a cheaper neighborhood; I canceled my cable subscription; I limited my data usage and calls and switched to a plan that cut my monthly bill by $30. . . . The next step was to figure out how to bring in extra income. So I followed my boyfriend's advice, putting my abundant energy into earning more money in any way that I could—from babysitting to focus groups to odd jobs. During this process, people at my company noticed what a hard worker I was, and I got five promotions, increasing my salary by $20,000.

With my cost cutting and extra income, I was able to reach my goal of putting $2,000 extra toward my debt each month. . . . Paying down my debt has changed the way that I see my money. As Rob and I start looking for a house, I now know there's a difference between what you can afford and what you can comfortably afford. I'll take the latter.   —Stephanie, 29, Washington, DC

"

Step 2. Face Facts

Next I suggest taking a look at **when you spent that money and what you spent it on,** so you can avoid this situation in the future. Is overspending something you do on autopilot? Studies have found that almost *half* of what we do every day is habit—no longer a decision we actively make. In his book *The Power of Habit*, Charles Duhigg explains that there are five types of cues that set off our bad choices: time of day, place, emotion, presence of specific people, and preceding behavior that is now a ritual.[13]

Was your debt precipitated by a big financial emergency (like being injured without health insurance or suddenly losing your job)? Or was it the result of many small bad habits? Do you always go on shopping binges on Saturdays to reward yourself for a hard week at work? Do you have a best friend who always encourages you to spend way beyond your means? Or are you simply accustomed to using your credit card for all of your wants, without regard to the bottom line of your bank account?

Whatever got you into this debt, take a moment to figure it out. And then forgive yourself. According to the *American Journal of Psychiatry*, roughly 5.8 percent of Americans shop compulsively.[14] The author of *I Shop Therefore I Am: Compulsive Buying and the Search for Self* suggests that one sign of a shopping addiction is when you shop to achieve a nonmaterial goal, as when you're using the act to feel fulfilled or to feel less lonely or because you're bored.[15] If you are vulnerable to these feelings, it doesn't mean you're a shopping addict; it just means you're human.

Believe it or not, approximately 40 percent of consumer spending is impulse buying; 88 percent of those purchases are made because the item is on sale.[16] And impulse buying seems to be on the rise, as smartphones make instant shopping easier than ever.[17]

There's no sense in dwelling on it or feeling paralyzed. Too many people I've met are frozen by anxiety or guilt over poor financial decisions. Acknowledge the mistakes you made in your past, then move forward and realize that a whole lot is within your control. You *can* change your habits over time. Losing debt is like losing weight: there's no instant fix, but some lifestyle changes and a good plan can get you where you need to be with minimal suffering.

Step 3. Stop Spending

Once you've acknowledged what got you into your current debt in the first place and vowed never to let it happen again, the next step to tackle your debt is to stop running it up by putting a total freeze on your credit-card spending. That may sound impossible to you right now, but it really isn't. You can pick one of two paths:

> **Option 1 A cash diet.** Allow yourself to spend only a certain amount of cash every week. When it runs out, that means you're done spending; it does *not* mean another trip to the ATM. Not only will this force you to plan ahead, but it also has the benefit of making every purchase more meaningful, as studies have shown it is psychologically harder to part with cash than to swipe your card.[18]

Option 2 A debit diet. Leave your credit cards at home and instead use your debit card for all purchases, making sure not to go over your weekly limit. **Double-check that you don't have "overdraft protection" on your debit card,** which could let you overdraw your account and rack up fees. The benefit here is that you can easily track everything you spend on a tool like LearnVest's Money Center. You can see what you're spending down to the dollar and avoid racking up more debt.

FEARLESS LESSON   *The Six Best Things to Pay for with a Credit Card*

If you tend to rack up credit-card debt and not pay it, then I recommend sticking to cash or debit cards, but if—*and only if*—you pay off your balance in full each month, credit cards can be a godsend. You can earn reward points that translate to actual cash savings, and you can have more consumer protection. Here are six areas where choosing the credit option can pay off big time.

1. **CAR RENTALS.** Credit cards often automatically provide some insurance coverage (call your credit-card company to check before renting). And most rental car agencies won't even take your debit card. Moreover, the few that do may perform a credit check in order to make sure you're a reliable consumer, which can cause your credit score to dip a few points due to the inquiry. If you want to use your debit card for a car rental, make sure to ask first if the rental agency requires a credit check. If it does, pay with your credit card instead.

2. **HOTELS.** When the front-desk hotel clerk asks for your credit or debit card when you check in, he's not just verifying your identity; he may be putting a hold on your account as a type of security deposit. This is to ensure that you have enough funds to cover the hotel stay. If the hold goes on your debit card, it will tie up the funds in your bank account for the entire duration of the stay. Choose instead to give him a spare credit card.

3. **ONLINE PURCHASES.** Unsecured online purchases with your debit card make you susceptible to theft. Your credit card likely offers better protection against fraudulent purchases than your debit card. If you're online shopping with your debit card while using an unsecured wireless Internet connection, as at a coffee shop (and who among us hasn't done that?), it's best to wait till you have a secure, trusted hookup. If you can't wait, use your credit card for the purchase.

4. **DELIVERIES.** Say you purchase a couch that will be delivered to your home in a few weeks, but it never comes. If you paid with your credit card, you're protected: a federal law called the Fair Credit Billing Act allows consumers to dispute various credit billing errors, including goods not delivered as agreed upon or damaged upon delivery. Debit cards and checks are not covered under this law.

5. **GAS.** Gas stations often don't encrypt your debit-card PIN. This means that if a thief can get into the pump, he can easily install a card-skimming device to collect your information. When you pull up to a gas station, consider using your credit card instead, which will make it easier to catch fraudulent charges and recoup losses. Also, avoid the pumps closest to the road; these lanes are most often targeted for skimming since they're farthest from the station clerk's view.

6. **RECURRING PAYMENTS.** How many recurring payments—like your gym membership, your Netflix account, your cell phone bill, your kid's glee club dues . . . the list goes on and on—get taken out of your debit account each month? One? Five? Ten? It can be easy to lose track. It's especially dangerous, though, if your recurring payments are put on your debit card; if your balance gets low, you'll have to pay overdraft fees. Unless you keep a generous cash buffer in your bank account, it's a good idea to put recurring payments on your credit card instead.

FEARLESS TIP *On the Rocks?*

When I tell you to freeze your credit card, I'm not kidding. Weight loss programs make you clean out your freezer and fridge. At LearnVest, we have another use for that freezer. If you're spending excessively, we suggest you put your credit card on ice . . . literally. When you have to break out the blow-dryer to melt a block of ice before you can buy anything on credit, it slows down your spending fast.

Step 4. Tally and Analyze Your Bad Debt

Okay, now that you've put a freeze on that debt (maybe literally), it's time to start paying it off. But first let's just get this all out there in the open. How much credit-card debt do you have? List the cards here, the balance owed, the minimum payments owed, and the APR for the card (look for it at the bottom of your monthly statement).

CREDIT-CARD DEBT

CARD NAME	BALANCE OWED	MINIMUM PAYMENT	APR
	*Total*_____	*Total*_____	

Total credit-card debt balance: $

Total minimum monthly credit-card payments: $

Do you have any other kinds of bad debt, like car loans, personal loans that are accruing interest, or back taxes owed?

OTHER DEBT

TYPE OF DEBT	BALANCE OWED	MINIMUM PAYMENT	INTEREST RATE
	Total	*Total*	

Total "other" debt balance: $

Total minimum monthly "other" payments: $

What is your bad-debt balance overall (add your total credit-card debt balance and total "other" debt balance)?: $

Even if that made you flinch, take a deep breath. You're going to be okay.

But before we can figure out your debt-repayment plan, we need to look at your current payment schedule.

What is the total of your minimum monthly
payments **due** (add your total minimum
monthly credit-card payments and
"other" payments)?: $

Keep this number in mind so you can avoid any delinquent
payments.

Step 5. Calculate How Much More You Can Afford to Repay

This is where the 50/20/30 method will really pay off.
Remember that you're in the chapter "The 20," so 20
percent or more of your take-home pay should be going
toward the goals in this chapter. You do have some competing goals here, so how much of that 20-plus percent
you dedicate to your debt repayment will vary based on
your personal situation. In general, though, high interest rates can
bump this goal into top priority, once you've covered retirement
contributions.

Talk to an

LV

Expert

FEARLESS TIP   *Split Your Payments*

While your credit-card statements typically show up once a month, your
credit-card interest is actually accruing on a daily basis. To help minimize
that pain, try splitting your payment amount in two so you can pay part of it
early in the month and the rest on the normal due date. You'll still be paying the same amount, but this can shave a little interest off and really helps
when your budget is tight!

Step 6. Negotiate Down Your Debt

Talking your way out of debt is like talking your way out of a
speeding ticket: sometimes it works and sometimes it doesn't, but
either way it doesn't really cost you anything except your breath.

To start, call each lender you owe money to, explain your situation (be sure to remind them what a loyal, longtime customer you've been), and see if they would be willing to lower your interest rate, waive some fees or penalties, or even cut down your balance. Lenders *want* you to repay them, so if you're more likely to pay them back at a lower interest rate, that's an incentive for them to help you.

If they turn you down the first time, keep calling back. The first person you talk to might not be able to help you, so ask to speak to a supervisor. If your finances have taken a dive recently and that's why you are struggling with this debt, you might even qualify for a hardship program, which would lower your interest rate, your minimum monthly payments, or both. If you've been getting offers from other companies for balance transfers or lower rates, mention those offers in your conversation—your bank won't want to lose your business. Also remember to stay calm, positive, and assertive. Steer clear of yes/no questions, which make it all too easy for them to deny you. Make this about what they can do for you.

Step 7. Make a Repayment Plan

Refer back to your list of debts on pages 134–35. Now put numbers next to each debt in order from highest APR to lowest. Once you handle your minimums across all cards, you should tackle your highest-interest cards first, one by one.

For example, let's say you have $8,000 in credit-card debt across five different cards. Each month, I recommend you first make the minimum payment for all five cards. Anything you've budgeted beyond that should go toward the balance on Card 1, which has the highest APR (and therefore racks up interest more quickly). After paying off Card 1, you would move on to the next one!

If you stick to your plan, we *will* get you there. One day at a time.

FEARLESS TIPS   *Unnecessary Banking Fees and How to Avoid Them*

If you're working hard to get rid of your credit-card debt, the last thing you need is to give more money to your bank! Here are a couple of tips to avoid those fees that will derail your get-out-of-debt efforts.

Tip 1   NEVER PAY FOR CHECKING. You should never, ever have to pay for your checking account. If you have a fee for checking now, check Bankrate.com for a better offer.

Tip 2   STAY AWAY FROM OVERDRAFT PROTECTION. If you're about to overdraw your account at an ATM, your bank will ask if you'd like to pay the $25 to $35 fee before allowing the transaction. My advice: Don't do it! A shady payday loan for $100 typically costs customers about $15 for two weeks of breathing room, an effective annual rate of 3.785 percent. The rate for a $35 overdraft fee on $100 is more than double that rate.[20] My advice is to avoid both. **If you need some breathing room, do a balance transfer.** If you just need to buy some time, a balance transfer credit card is probably a better option than overdraft protection. And if that's too much, any credit card you transfer the balance to will still give you a month of leeway to get you to that next paycheck. Just be careful not to overdo it, because you won't get that ATM overdraft warning when you swipe a credit card.

Step 8. Consider a Balance Transfer

In the wake of the recession, it was harder to get good introductory credit-card offers, but in 2011 they made a comeback, paving the way for easier balance transfers.[21] A balance transfer simply means you move your balance from one credit card to another with a lower APR. Sound too good to be true? Well, **there are pros and cons.** If you think you can pay your debt off in just a few months or your current interest rates are less than 10 percent, this step probably isn't worth your time. That's because cards often charge balance transfer fees (the catch!), which could be more than the interest you will save. If your debt repayment will take longer and you have a high interest rate, use Bankrate.com to search for credit cards that offer the opportunity to transfer to a card with a lower or 0 percent interest rate. Comparison shop for the best card, looking at these factors:

- **Balance transfer fees.** These fees are a percentage of the debt being transferred, typically around 3 percent.[22]

- **Introductory interest rates.** These are usually 0 percent to entice you to transfer your debt. Warning: they typically reset at very steep rates (up to 22.99 percent after a number of months!).[23]

- **Regular interest rates.** These are the interest rates you'll get after the introductory period is over. Pay particular attention to this number (often buried in the fine print), as you don't want to get stuck paying more interest than you would have if you'd kept your debt where it was.

FEARLESS LESSON   *Watch Out for Accrued Interest*

If you don't think you can pay off your credit card before the introductory period ends, don't sign up for a card that charges accrued interest. When the intro period ends, you'll have to pay the regular interest rate on your *entire* transfer—not just what you have left to pay. You know, when things seem too good to be true, they usually are, so *always* read the fine print, and if you're unsure what it means, ask for more info.

The higher your credit score, the easier it will be to find a balance transfer offer with especially good terms. Now let's look at an example to see how this could pay off.

BALANCE TRANSFER BREAKDOWN	
Debt to be transferred	$3,000
Interest you'd pay in a year with your old card	$334.84
0% introductory period on new card	12 months
Credit limit on new card	$3,500
Can you transfer the whole debt?	Yes, the debt is less than the credit-card limit.
Interest you pay with new card	$0, as long as you pay off the debt within a year.
Transfer fee	3%, with a minimum of $75
What fee must you pay?	$90
Total savings from transfer	$244.84 (interest savings of $334.84 minus $90 fee)*

*Note that you must pay off your credit card ASAP within the introductory period so you can get those savings *before* the interest rate resets to something higher.

FEARLESS LESSON   *My Rules for Balance Transfers*

Rule 1   Aim to make only one transfer onto this card, while the APR is 0 percent to 3 percent.

Rule 2   Never make a single purchase on this card. Ever. The only purpose of this new card is to help carry some of your debt at a lower interest rate, *not* to add to your current debt! You're on a cash diet, remember?

Rule 3   If you still have a large balance on your old card after the introductory rate expires on the new one, it's okay to try one more balance transfer—as long as you never (ever) exceed one balance transfer in a year. Opening up lots of new credit in a short time period can have a negative impact on your credit score.

Rule 4   Set up automatic payments for this new credit card. The minimum on your old card should go down after the transfer, so put that extra money toward paying off the balance on this new card. Pay it off aggressively.

Note that there is a bit of risk to this strategy: if you apply for new credit cards and get declined, it can lower your credit score. Applying for a card counts as a hard inquiry, and if you aren't given the line of credit, your credit score may take a hit. In this economy, balance transfers and low-interest credit cards are increasingly hard to come by, so it's a bit of a catch-22: people who already have strong credit scores will have the best luck. Balance transfers can be a great option, so if you receive something in the mail saying that you've been preapproved, consider yourself lucky. Otherwise, you can still give this technique a shot—just know that it's not entirely without risk.

FEARLESS TIP *Investigate Personal Loans*

In addition to balance transfers, a personal loan from a bank or credit union can be another way to pay off absurdly high-interest-rate cards with a fixed and lower-rate loan. But note: this *only* works when you use 100 percent of the loan toward the debts you already owe. It is not an excuse to rack up more debt!

Step 9. Consider Credit Counseling (If You're Too Far Underwater)

Buyer beware! There are *so* many credit-consolidating scams out there. But it's actually possible to get credit counseling for free via the National Foundation for Credit Counseling.* If you need someone to help you sort out your credit options, go there first. Counselors will help you figure out a payment plan, provide confidential budget advice, negotiate reduced payments to your

* Note: Although the initial counseling session will be free, the debt-management plan is not. The NFCC does not actually do the counseling itself; instead, it directs you to a nonprofit credit counselor for your situation. Those companies tend to charge fees for their services, so you might pay $20 to $50 per month on top of your debt payments.[24]

lender, and sometimes prevent your creditors from taking legal action. You can find more info at www.nfcc.org.

FEARLESS LESSON   *The Debt Collector*

Getting a call from a debt collector can be terrifying. It's important to know that you have rights, thanks to the Fair Debt Collection Practices Act. A collector must send you a written "validation notice," telling you how much money you owe and to whom, within five days after he first contacts you. Collectors can't harass you, make false statements, misrepresent the amount you owe, use profanity, contact you at work without permission, or give false credit info about you to anyone. (Note that these rules don't cover debts you've incurred from running a business.) If you have any problems with a debt collector, contact your state's attorney general's office and the Federal Trade Commission.

The Final Step . . .

Remember, when you understand the psychology behind your spending habits, it's a lot easier to start making better, more informed decisions about where your money goes. So take a hard look at yourself and figure out what may be driving your debt-incurring ways. Whatever your goals and obstacles, know that you have the *power* to get out of debt and stay there!

What You've Accomplished

✓ Analyzed how you got into credit-card debt

✓ Halted your credit-card spending and started a cash or debit diet

✓ Put your credit cards on ice (literally)

✓ Set up a direct deposit into your freedom fund account

✓ Put a plan in place to build up this account quickly (from cutting costs to earning extra income on the side)

Questions for Your Expert

If you still have questions about anything we've covered in this section, write them here and then go to www.learnvest.com/financiallyfearless for answers.

I still don't understand . . .

_____

_____

Talk to an

LV

Expert

Where do I find . . .

_____

_____

What should I do about my . . .

_____

_____

Examples:

How do I start to build up my credit again after getting out of debt?

If I have a credit card with a good rewards program, should I still freeze it?

Which card should I close?

How can I fix my credit score?

Student Loans

Let's be clear about one thing. Even though I told you good debt is better than bad debt, it doesn't mean it's something you actually want hanging over your head. No matter how "good" a debt is, you still have to pay it off. I consider student loans "good debt" because they are an investment in your future and can up your earning power. Even though this debt was a means to an end, it can still be a cause of stress. Just because education has a higher return on investment than stocks or bonds[25] doesn't mean that having hundreds of thousands in good debt feels *awesome*.

If you're saddled with student debt, it's important to realize that you aren't alone. Nearly 70 percent of us graduate with student loans—on average more than $25,000 worth and plenty of us to the tune of five or even six figures.[26] It's staggering to think that so many of us enter the real world with as much debt as our starting salaries. As a nation, our collective student-loan debt has topped $1 trillion (yes, *trillion*).[27]

We're in the midst of a student-loan crisis. To start, the cost of education is rapidly rising. According to the *New York Times*, college tuition and fees are 559 percent of what they were in 1985.

Consumer prices have about doubled, but college costs have sextupled![28] Meanwhile, the job market is tighter. In 2011, over 53 percent of those twenty-five and under with a bachelor's degree were underemployed or altogether unemployed.[29]

No surprise, then, that people are defaulting like crazy. According to the U.S. Department of Education,[30] the default rate is about 13 percent overall. Default rates for student loans at for-profit schools are at almost 23 percent! And since you can't discharge student-loan debt in bankruptcy, you're pretty much stuck with it.

According to the *New York Times*, most experts agree that student debt hangs "like a dark cloud" over the economic recovery, causing people to delay things like buying a home, saving for retirement (clearly they haven't read this book), starting a family, and achieving financial security.[31] Yes, student debt is a huge problem, but luckily, with a plan, you can find a solution.

How Do You Get Rid of Student Debt?

Granted, student debt can be a real problem, but it doesn't need to be a financial life sentence. There are ways to get rid of it for good. The first step is to figure out what kind of loan you have.

Um, What Loans Did I Take Out Again?

You can look yours up in the National Student Loan Data System (http://www.nslds.ed.gov) using your Social Security number, your date of birth, and your PIN provided to you by the Department of Education. If you don't know your PIN, you can apply for one at http://www.pin.ed.gov/. If you don't find yourself in the database, yours is probably a private loan.

If you have subsidized federal loans. For those of you just out of school thinking, *I have to start paying it off now? I don't even have a job!* there's some good news. For most federal loans, you have a grace period of six months from the time you graduate or drop below half-time enrollment before you need to start repaying your loans.[32] More good news: during this time the government is paying your interest and you have forty-five days after the grace period ends to make your first payment. (If you have a PLUS loan, you do not get a grace period.)

Keep in mind, though, that you'll need to start making payments once the grace period is over or run the risk of going into default.

If you have private or unsubsidized loans. For unsubsidized loans and private loans, the interest starts accruing as soon as the loan is disbursed, or given to you—yes, that means before you even graduate. That cost of interest can be significant, though it is generally less than credit-card debt. If you have an unsubsidized or PLUS loan, it may make sense to make even small payments while you're in school to combat some of this growing interest.

FEDERAL	
Direct subsidized loans and subsidized federal Stafford loans (aka subsidized loans)	The benefit of subsidized loans is that the federal government pays the interest on them while you are enrolled at least half time in school, during the six-month grace period after you graduate (during which you don't have to make payments on your loan), and during deferment periods.
Direct unsubsidized loans and unsubsidized federal Stafford loans (aka unsubsidized loans)	You are responsible for paying the interest on unsubsidized loans starting from the date you received the loan—whether that is during your grace period, while you're enrolled, or while the loan is in deferment.
Direct PLUS loans and federal PLUS loans	These loans are for graduate or professional-degree students or for parents of dependent undergraduate students. As with unsubsidized loans, you are responsible for paying the interest from the date you receive the loan, regardless of whether you're in a grace period, are enrolled, or have the loan in deferment.
Federal Family Education Loan	The FFEL program halted giving out student loans in 2010, but it's very possible you have a holdover. FFELs were given by private lenders but backed by the federal government, with the same repayment options and protections as federal loans.

PRIVATE
Private loans are governed by a different set of rules (mainly the lenders') from federal loans. They can come from banks, schools, nonprofit institutions, or other lenders. Note that while Sallie Mae is technically a government-backed entity, loans through this lender function as private loans.

All About Repayment Plans

If you don't communicate with your federal lender, you'll be automatically enrolled in a standard payment plan (see page 148). But you actually have other options for federal loans, depending on how many years you want to have to pay your loans off and what your income looks like. Overall, the most important thing to keep in mind is that the lower you make your monthly payments and the longer you take to pay off your loan, **the more you will pay in interest over the lifetime of the loan.**

Standard repayment plan. You pay a fixed amount of at least $50 a month for up to ten years. Compared to the following repayment plans, this option tends to provide the best value for most people (aside from just paying off your loan right now), as you will pay the least interest over the life of the loan.

Graduated repayment plan. This is best for people who have a low income now but expect it to gradually rise, as payments start out low and increase every two years. You have up to ten years to pay. Because interest accumulates faster in the early years, you'll pay more overall for your loan under this plan than under the standard plan, because for the first few years, you are essentially just paying interest instead of paying off the loan itself. If you are in this type of plan and don't send more than the interest you owe every month, then **you are not getting any closer to paying off your loan**—you're just paying to have the loan not go into default.

Extended repayment plan. If you have more than $30,000 in Direct or FFEL loans, you could qualify for the extended repayment plan, which gives you twenty-five years to pay off your loans. Note that if you have both Direct and FFEL loans but hold over $30,000 in only one type, you can get the extended repayment plan only for that type. For example, if you have $40,000 in Direct loans and $25,000 in FFEL loans, you can apply the extended repayment program only to the Direct loans. While your monthly payments will be lower—because you are spreading out repayment over a longer period of time—you'll also pay more in interest over the life of the loan.

Income-based, income-sensitive, or income-contingent repayment plans. These repayment plans really only differ in which kind of loans they apply to. Your payment is capped at a number that is affordable to you based on your income. The repayment period is up to twenty-five years. If by then you still have a loan balance, it may be forgiven (but you may have to pay income tax on the forgiven portion).

An income-based repayment plan is an especially good choice if you are enrolled in a program for people working in public service or teaching jobs that forgives your loans after ten years, called Public Service Loan Forgiveness (PSLF). This will keep your payments affordable until that time when you can stop making them altogether![33]

Want to Have Your Student Debt Forgiven?

The Public Service Loan Forgiveness program applies to Direct loans only. Essentially, if you've already made 120 payments on your loan and you work in certain public-service fields, you may be eligible to have the remainder forgiven. Visit http://www.studentaid.ed.gov/repay-loans/forgiveness-cancellation/charts/public-service for all the details on how to qualify. It's relatively complicated, so **make sure you keep track of your qualifying service** on a regular basis using the form the Federal Student Aid office provides so that it's not a huge task once you've reached your qualifying time frame.

There are also magical-seeming loan "forgiveness" programs. But don't get your hopes up: you can only cancel your loan in very limited circumstances (usually even declaring bankruptcy doesn't do it), like if your school was improperly certified or if you die (not worth it).

Your repayment options vary for private loans, and some private lenders don't offer any repayment options other than the standard one. You should contact your private lender to find out if you have options.

The good news is that, as of 2008, you can pay off as much of your loans as you want early, with no penalty, whether they are public or private. You can also request a shorter payment schedule.

Doing either of these things will save you money, because you will accrue less interest.

FEARLESS TIPS   *Repaying Your Loans*

Tip 1   **TACKLE YOUR PRINCIPAL.** Anytime you pay more than the minimum on your student loan, keep in mind that excess payments will be applied first to interest and then to principal. If the additional payment is greater than one monthly installment, **you *should* include a note with the payment telling the processor you want it to be treated as a reduction of principal.** Otherwise, the processor will treat it as though you paid the next payment early, and you won't be making the dent in your principal that you could be making (thereby lowering future interest payments).

Tip 2   **REAP THE TAX BENEFITS.** Don't forget to deduct your student-loan interest come tax time! **You can deduct $2,500 (that's the 2013 amount) or the total amount you paid in student-loan interest,** whichever is less (as long as your income is below the IRS limits). Deductions allow you to decrease your tax liability, which is a good trade-off for having to pay interest in the first place.

Tip 3   **BE REWARDED.** There are a few loan rewards programs out there that you should know about. Check out SmarterBucks (www.smarterbucks.com) and the Upromise Loan Link Program by Sallie Mae (www.salliemae.com/landing /upromise/loanlink/default.aspx), both of which allow you to apply rewards from everyday spending toward your student-loan payments.

Which Loan Should I Pay Off First?

Okay, so you have multiple loans and no clue which to pay off first. Don't worry, these rules of thumb can help. If you have private student loans, I'd focus on paying those off first while making the minimum payments on your federal loans. There are two reasons for this:

- In 2013 interest rates are low, but because most private loans have variable interest rates, your private loan could—and most likely will—rise in the future.

- Private lenders aren't obligated to work with you in financial duress, while federal loan servicers are. If you get hit with a job loss or other financial emergency, having your private loans paid off and only federal loans remaining gives you more flexibility with payments. Plus, private loans are not forgivable upon death, so the sooner they're paid off, the better.

After you pay off your private loans, you should order your remaining federal loans from highest to lowest interest rate and focus on paying the high-interest loans off first.

Should You Consolidate Your Student Loans?

Consolidating loans allows you to take all of your smaller loans and combine them into one, called a *consolidation loan*. If you do this, then you'll be able to pay back all of your loans in one monthly payment—which will help you keep track of your expenses. If you consolidate your loans, you may also have new opportunities to defer your loans. You can also sign up for different repayment plans, which is helpful if you need to restructure your current schedule. Once you do the complicated math, the amount of interest you pay over time will be about the same, since combining all your loans combines all your interest rates. The catch is you'll lose any grace period (if any remains), which means you'll need to start repaying right away. You'll also lose subsidized benefits and, as a result of the subprime mortgage crisis, it's now more difficult to consolidate smaller loan amounts.

Alert: if a company promises to significantly reduce monthly payments, it may just be stretching out your loan period, requiring you to pay more interest over time.

Remember . . . if you don't understand something or are having trouble with your payments, don't hesitate to contact your loan servicer. Read all communications from your loan holder and keep all your records pertaining to your loans in a safe place. Prioritize making your payments on time and in full. It's challenging, but hey, you're up for a challenge, right? You went to college, after all.

Talk to an

LV

Expert

Should You Go Back to School?

When you're sitting in a cold, sterile cubicle, the thought of strolling across a quad, backpack slung over your shoulder, autumn leaves swirling around you, can have the effect of a fever dream. But you need to separate your fantasy of college life—whether that's *Revenge of the Nerds, Felicity,* or *Legally Blonde*—from the reality of going back to school, which in many cases will prove even more of a slog than the job you fled for it. For some, going back to school is a strategic maneuver to increase earning power; for others, it's a stopgap measure (or some might say procrastination technique) to delay deciding what to do as an adult. Going back to school makes more sense during certain stages in your financial life than others. If you're grappling with this decision, check out our Grad School Calculator at www.learnvest.com/financially fearless.

FEARLESS TIPS *How to Stay Debt Free If You're Going to College (or Grad School) Now*

Tip 1 PURSUE ALL POSSIBLE GRANTS, SCHOLARSHIPS, AND FINANCIAL AID. Fill out your FAFSA (Free Application for Federal Student Aid) even if you don't think you qualify. You can search for grants and scholarships by using a free service like Fastweb, Scholarships.com, FindTuition.com,

ScholarshipExperts.com, or Sallie Mae's College Answer. Applying may take some time, but it is worth it for literally free money.

Tip 2   **FOR COLLEGE, CONSIDER STATE SCHOOLS.** You can often get a great education for far less at a state school than at a private or out-of-state college. Check out the college rankings by *U.S. News & World Report*, which has a handy "Best Value" sort button on its website (colleges.usnews.rankingsandreviews.com) and a list of the best public schools.

Tip 3   **FOR GRAD SCHOOL, CALCULATE YOUR LIKELY STARTING SALARY AND MONTHLY STUDENT-LOAN PAYMENTS OUT OF SCHOOL AND MAKE SURE THEY MAKE SENSE BASED ON WHAT SALARY YOU CAN EXPECT.** If you know what field you want to go into, it's easy enough to go online and find a ballpark estimate of what you can expect to be paid (try Salary.com, Glassdoor.com, and PayScale.com). If you're only going to be making $22,000 and that master's in comparative literature is costing you $1,200 a month, you're looking at more ramen noodles than any adult should have to eat. Most grad schools will give you a sense of what average salaries their graduates make.

Tip 4   **MAX OUT YOUR FEDERAL LOAN OPTIONS BEFORE PURSUING PRIVATE LOANS.** Private lenders like Sallie Mae typically have higher interest rates.

Tip 5   **TRY TO AVOID HAVING YOUR PARENTS COSIGN UNLESS THEY ARE DEFINITELY IN A POSITION TO HELP YOU OUT IF YOU NEED THEM TO.** Otherwise, if neither of you can pay the loan after you graduate, you'll tank *everyone's* credit.

Tip 6   **BE WARY OF ONLINE DEGREES.** Flexible academic programs can seem tempting now that you're not a kid anymore, but a lot of online programs are bogus. Do your research and don't get scammed.

Student-Loan Lingo You Should Know

LOAN PRINCIPAL. This is the initial amount you borrowed, which doesn't include interest you've been charged. For example, if you take out a loan for $10,000, the principal is $10,000. You might owe more to the lender, however, because of interest charged over time.

INTEREST. What you "pay" for taking out the loan. Interest—ranging from 3 percent to 18 percent of the loan—is calculated daily and added to the balance of what you owe the lender. The longer you take to pay back the loan, the more interest you will pay overall.

GRACE PERIOD. For certain federal student loans, the six-month period after graduation or after dropping below half-time enrollment before a borrower must start making payments.

CONSOLIDATION. Combining several loans into one loan requiring one monthly payment. Often consolidation spreads out repayment of all the loans over a longer period of time.

CAPITALIZED INTEREST. Interest accrued during a period when a student-loan holder isn't required to make payments—either because she is in school or because the student loan is in the grace period or deferment. It is added to the principal of the loan.

I know that paying off your student loans may not be your number one financial priority, and the amount you'll be able to put toward them each month might vary depending on what else you have going on. Still, I'd recommend putting as much of your 20 toward it as possible, so you can start putting your money toward saving for other future goals . . . like your kid's college fund.

What You've Accomplished

✓ Looked up your loans on the National Student Loan Data System

✓ Considered your repayment-plan options

✓ Set a calendar reminder to deduct your student-loan interest come tax time

✓ Established a plan to pay off private loans first (while making minimum payments on federal loans)

✓ Considered consolidating your loans

Questions for Your Expert

If you still have questions about anything we've covered in this section, write them here and then go to www.learnvest.com/financiallyfearless for answers.

I still don't understand . . .

_____

_____

Where do I find . . .

Talk to an

LV

Expert

_____

_____

What should I do about my . . .

_____

_____

Examples:

I still can't decide whether or not to consolidate. I have three different loan payments every month—is it worth it?

If I already have a repayment plan in place, where do I go to change it?

Mortgages

Before you start the process of getting a mortgage, I strongly encourage you to consult a financial planner. In general, anytime you are making a major financial decision, I believe it's worth the few hundred dollars to talk to an expert. That goes for starting a small business, investing in your brother's friend's girlfriend's artistic project, or making any major purchase, like a plot of land. When it comes to buying a home, a financial planner can help you get the information you need and can be a realistic, calming presence in a sometimes-confusing process. This may be the biggest purchase you'll make in your life. **It's essential that you get it right.**

To Buy or Not to Buy

How important is it to you to own your own home? A Better Homes and Gardens Real Estate survey found that 75 percent of Gen X-ers and Gen Y-ers surveyed believed that owning a nice home was a key indicator of success.[34] Certainly, buying a home can be a great accomplishment. And yes, even if you do have to take out a hefty mortgage, this does count as good debt since a home is an investment that will appreciate in value (despite temporary dips) over the long run. However, it's not something I would recommend doing until your financial foundation is solid.

As you debate whether it makes sense to buy or continue renting, consider whether you're planning to keep the house for five years or more. When factoring in closing costs and real estate fees, that's about how long it takes for buying to really pay off.[35]

If you decide to buy, a mortgage is an obvious piece of the puzzle. If done right, a mortgage can help you turn your home into an asset with the potential for growth. It can add to your financial portfolio, give you a big tax break, and, of course, provide you with a place to live.

But as we've seen in the recent housing crisis, there are dangers. It is so important not to get in over your head. With the abundant news of foreclosures fresh in our minds, let's make sure you are *really* ready before you buy. There are so many variables in how much the whole experience will cost. Some have to do with your desirability as a borrower. But a lot hinges on how savvy you are. For example, it helps to know how to negotiate title insurance, closing costs, attorney fees, and mortgage rates. In this section, I'll take you step by step through the mortgage process.

Step 1. Figure Out How Much Home You Can Afford

This is arguably *the* most important step. If you buy a home that you can only barely afford and then something happens to your income, you will find yourself in a world of hurt. **This is the biggest mistake I see first-time home buyers make!**

Start by looking at how much you have saved for a down payment. Do you have 20 percent or more socked away for a house of your target price? Most lenders prefer that an applicant borrow no more than 80 percent of the cost of the house. If you can't pay that much, you may still qualify for a mortgage, but you might pay a higher interest rate. And keep in mind that if the housing market dips, the fact that you have so little equity in the house will give you little to no cushion to absorb any loss that you might incur if you have to move.

Don't forget to factor in homeowner's association fees, property taxes, and homeowner's insurance—all of which could quickly turn a $3,000 monthly mortgage payment into a $4,500 monthly expense. Remember that overall you'll want your mortgage payment, including taxes and insurance, to be about 30 percent of your income (and certainly *well* under 50 percent).

Note: You should **not** take your down payment out of your freedom fund or, worse, out of a 401(k) or other retirement account.

Step 2. Check Your Credit Score and Credit Report

When you apply for a mortgage, your lender will need to see evidence that you're a reliable borrower. If you're planning to apply for a mortgage in the near future, you probably won't have time to improve your credit score, but you'll want to make sure that there aren't any errors on your report. In the world of mortgages, a score over 720 is considered strong; under 660 is looked upon as weak, which may mean that you'll have to pay a higher interest rate.

FEARLESS TIP   *Keep a Credit Report on Hand*

Save a copy of your credit report so that each lender doesn't have to perform a hard inquiry.

To see real examples of how your credit score can affect your mortgage APR check out this chart (which assumes a thirty-year fixed mortgage, based on the national average of a $300,000 loan).

FICO SCORE	APR	MONTHLY PAYMENT
760–850	3.707%	$1,382
700–759	3.929%	$1,420
680–699	4.106%	$1,451
660–679	4.320%	$1,488
640–659	4.750%	$1,565
620–639	5.296%	$1,665

Source: myfico.com (as of June 12, 2013).

Step 3. Assemble Your Financial Documents and Your Down Payment

Be prepared to get financially naked. The bank is going to look at *all* previous financial records—everything from student debts to outstanding medical bills to missed credit-card payments—so you'll want to get ready to bare all. Lenders almost always require applicants to do the following:

- Verify income, which you can usually do by presenting recent pay stubs—or tax returns if you're self-employed.

- Show how much cash (money not tied up in investments) you have available to spend. Postrecession, lenders are extremely cautious about liquidity, so it's not unusual for a lender to require that you have several months' worth of mortgage payments in the bank. Your bank statements can serve as proof of your liquid assets.

- Disclose other assets you own (real estate, investment accounts, cars, etc.) and all of your debts, including personal loans, credit cards, and student loans.

To prepare months in advance, I suggest that you pay off any credit-card balances and make sure to stay below 30 percent utilization on any card you're still using. Also make sure you can account for any transfer between bank accounts and the sources of all deposits. And start liquidating whatever portion of your brokerage assets will be converted into a down payment, especially since you can ease into this over the next few months. (An FDIC-insured money-market account is a simple safe haven, but be sure to stay under FDIC limits in one single bank account!) This prevents you from having to do a fire sale if markets dip but the time is right to buy that apartment, and it protects these dollars from the risk of the capital markets.

FEARLESS LESSON   *What You Need to Know About the FDIC*

The FDIC—Federal Deposit Insurance Corporation—protects your money if your insured bank fails. If your bank goes under with your cash, you can get back up to $250,000 per account type, per person, per insured bank. The account types that qualify are an individual account (e.g., a savings account in your name only), a joint account (e.g., a savings account you and your spouse share), a retirement account (e.g., an IRA), and a trust account (e.g., a revocable trust). So if you are buying a big house and working with that much money, you want to make sure you're not leaving a huge lump sum—say $500,000—in an individual account. You'll need to diversify! If this applies to you, check out fdic.gov for more details.

Step 4. Consider Whether You Need a Mortgage Broker

A mortgage broker's job is to act as an intermediary between you and a lender. A broker will help you figure out what types of mortgages you qualify for and who offers them. A broker's chief advantage is insider knowledge of the industry, plus his or her relationships with lenders. If a broker brings a lender enough business, that lender might be inclined to help him (and you!) more. However, since lenders usually pay brokers, the lender might increase your interest rate to accommodate that extra cost. A 2008 study by the U.S. Department of Housing and Urban Development found that buyers who worked with a broker paid, on average, $300 to $425 more in fees than borrowers who did not work with brokers.[36]

If you have the time and the patience to approach lenders yourself, working without a broker can be the more affordable option if you know what you're doing. You can check out your local bank, which may serve as a good resource for a mortgage loan. If you have excellent credit, the bank may lend you the money and hold the loan "in house," meaning that it will act as both broker and lender. The bank may also make the loan to you initially and then sell your loan to a larger bank or mortgage lender. This is common, and the terms of your original loan will still be in place. After all, a loan is a contract, and whoever buys the contract is still bound to honor it.

FEARLESS LESSON *What Are "Points"?*

Points are a form of prepaid interest and are paid at closing; 1 point is generally equal to 1 percent of the loan amount (not the purchase price of the home). By prepaying interest, you are generally able to get a lower interest rate for the life of the loan, which means potentially paying less in overall interest.

If you can afford to pay the points in addition to your down payment, this may be a good option. But if you're trying to keep your up-front costs as low as possible, go for a zero-point option.

Step 5. Look for a Lender with a Reputation for Good Customer Service, Timely Mortgage Closings, and Competitive Rates

When you make an offer on a house, you are entering into a legal contract that carries various contingencies, including a set date and time to close. A delayed closing can cost hundreds of dollars a day in penalties and can even put you at risk of the sale falling through. For this reason, when you look for a lender, you'll want to make sure you go with someone reliable. If you're already working with a real estate agent, ask for a recommendation. Also speak to friends and family who've bought homes recently for suggestions.

The next step I recommend is to make calls directly to lenders and to your local bank. It's a good idea to make these calls in one fell swoop. Rates change daily, so calling different lenders on different days may not give you an accurate idea of comparative rates.

When you contact a lender, don't offer up your Social Security number. **Instead, give your credit score and income and ask for a quote.** This quote won't be exact, since the lender will revise it once it has more information. To make the comparison easier, ask for the rates on one specific type of mortgage, such as the common thirty-year fixed. And keep in mind that major banks aren't the only institutions that can grant mortgages. Credit and labor unions sometimes also offer mortgages, and if you qualify, there are special arrangements for veterans. Government loans are available through the Federal Housing Administration, but the availability of loans varies depending on where you live. If you think that you might qualify, you can view the requirements on the FHA website (FHA.gov).

Make sure to exhaust your options before choosing a lender. While it's obviously important to find a lender that can offer a low interest rate, it's crucial to find one that is also trustworthy with a good reputation. If you find a lender with interest rates too good to be true, they probably are just that.

FEARLESS LESSON   *How Mortgages Are Structured*

With a mortgage, you'll pay the principal, interest, taxes, and insurance—all of which are commonly referred to as PITI. Note that paying taxes and insurance separately from your mortgage will mean a lower mortgage payment. Just remember that it's up to you to save that money month to month so you can pay the annual bill when it comes! Banks largely prefer to collect the tax and insurance money in an account held by a third party (called escrow) because they pay only a little to maintain the account and have access to those funds. This is called "impounding" and is designed to protect you from having to pay a large property tax or insurance bill all at once. Here's how each component works:

ESCROW. A bank account held by a third party to keep money safe before a deal is finalized or "closed"; also used for holding payments earmarked for annual expenses.

P PRINCIPAL. The original amount that you borrowed to buy your home.

I INTEREST. The amount of money you pay back to the bank on top of what you borrowed. When you take out a mortgage, you agree to an interest rate, which will determine how much you pay a lender to keep lending. It's expressed as a percentage: 3 percent to 4 percent is considered somewhat standard as of 2013, but the rates depend strongly on a person's situation—income and credit—as evaluated by the lender.

T TAXES. Property taxes go toward supporting city, school district, county, and/or state infrastructure, and you can pay them along with your mortgage. They're calculated as a percentage of your property value, so you can roughly estimate what you'll pay by searching public records for the property taxes paid on nearby homes of similar value.

I INSURANCE. Any payments reserved for homeowner's insurance to protect against fire, theft, or other disasters are held in an escrow account. You also may be required to have private mortgage insurance (PMI), which helps guarantee that the lender will get its money back if you can't pay it for any reason. After you've paid off a certain amount of your mortgage, you're sometimes allowed to cancel the PMI (although this depends on your situation), or if the market appreciates quickly, you may be able to refinance so that you can eliminate the PMI. Remember that PMI is meant to protect the lender, not the borrower—so it won't bail you out if you default on your payments.

Step 6. Choose the Mortgage That's Right for You

Mortgages aren't one-size-fits-all. The payment plans vary by interest rate and by duration—the most popular plans offer a fixed rate (meaning the interest rate will always be the same) for fifteen, twenty, or thirty years. The other option is an adjustable rate, which means that the interest rate will change each year. Loans can be fixed, adjustable, or a combination of the two. Here's how to choose:

An **adjustable-rate mortgage (ARM)** is one in which the interest rate changes at preset intervals to reflect the current market. This type may be ideal if any of these circumstances apply:

- You are primarily looking for low interest rates in the short term (say, you're expecting a big pay raise within the next five years and will be able to pay higher interest).

- You don't intend to stay in the home long enough for rates to rise (say, you're planning to renovate and flip the house).

- You plan to refinance or have your loan reevaluated for a potentially better rate before the rate becomes adjustable.

Note: **You should be wary of adjustable rates,** as you take on the risk of being reset out of your price range. This is just another variable to be careful about. To mitigate the risk, find out what the maximum rate reset amount is each year.

A **fixed-rate mortgage** is one in which you pay a fixed interest rate for the duration of the mortgage. It may be ideal if any one of these is true:

- Interest rates are rising.

- You're counting on a steady, predictable payment.

- You plan to stay in the home for a long time (which in general is when it makes sense to buy a home).

There are also **interest-only loans,** which allow you to pay only the interest on the loan for an initial period of time (usually ten years). Since you are not paying any principal the payments are lower, but more interest will be paid in the long run with this kind of loan, since it takes longer to repay the principal. After the initial period expires, you may choose to enter into another interest-only loan, pay off the principal, or convert the loan to a principal plus interest loan.

FEARLESS LESSON   *The Housing Bubble: What the Hell Happened?*

You know there was a major housing market collapse in 2007–2008, but do you know all the factors that led to it? We can't have amnesia about crises like this. Here's a quick summary:

1. **MORTGAGE FRAUD.** In the early 2000s, some lenders gave what are known as "subprime" mortgage loans to people who couldn't afford them. When the buyers couldn't keep up on the payments, their homes went into foreclosure.[37]

2. **SPECULATION.** Developers built tons of condos, especially in California, Florida, Arizona, and Nevada, without planning to own them long term, and when the bottom fell out, they were left holding a lot of property that wasn't worth as much as they thought it would be.[38]

3. **UNEMPLOYMENT.** The real estate market is often tied to employment. So when jobs go by the wayside, the housing market can fall apart, too.[39]

Step 7. Get Preapproved

In the preapproval process, a reputable mortgage lender will agree to give you a mortgage loan for a specified amount, but you won't make a commitment to buy a specific property. You'll fill out a full mortgage application, which will ask you about your comprehensive financial history. You'll also usually pay an application fee, so don't take this step unless you're truly ready to start shopping for a home. In some cases, you won't even need to meet with your lender to submit the application. The lender will let you send it via e-mail.

Preapproval used to be less common, but it's now expected that you'll get preapproved before you even start house hunting. Not only does it improve your chances of getting the seller to take your offer seriously, but it will also make the final mortgage process move more quickly once you've agreed to a price. There are two caveats: First, just because you are preapproved for a certain amount of debt doesn't mean that you should necessarily borrow that much. Remember that you want to keep your housing payments to about 30 percent of your take-home pay. Second, preapproval letters do not last forever, so it's not something that you want to do too early in the process. They usually need to be drawn up for each offer you make, and the lender will likely ask you for updated documentation all the way through the close of the loan to reverify the information that you provided to confirm that your financial situation hasn't changed.

Step 8. Ask for an Estimate of Closing Costs

Before you sign a contract for the purchase of your home, ask the lender for a "good-faith estimate." Your lender will estimate how much money you'll need for closing costs, which are the extra charges and fees you'll be asked to pay when you finally become the owner of the house. Closing costs can include points, taxes, title insurance, financing costs, and more. The lender will also look at your bank accounts to ensure that you have enough socked away for the cost of the actual move.

In some instances, a motivated seller will offer to pay your closing costs just to get the deal done. Although this may seem like a good thing, it may mean that the seller is less willing to budge on the sale price and you're really just amortizing the cost into your thirty-year mortgage. Try to get both the lower sale price and the closing costs taken care of.

Finally, I recommend doing a home inspection during closing (including a roof inspection). I also recommend a home warranty policy before you close—this protects all the major (and expensive-to-repair) appliances, heating system, etc. For a free-standing home (i.e., not an apartment), you should also consider a roof warranty.

Step 9. Consider What You'll Do If You Get Rejected

Let's say that you've done your research, figured out how much you can afford, decided whether you need a broker, found a trustworthy lender, chosen the mortgage structure that's best for you, and submitted your paperwork . . . but the lender says, "Not so fast!" Even if you've done everything right, it doesn't necessarily mean that you'll get the mortgage you want. Lending requirements have tightened *significantly* since the housing crisis, and you can expect lenders to follow strict approval guidelines. There's a good chance you'll be approved for a smaller mortgage than the one you applied for, which means that you'll need to either rethink the house you had intended to buy and bid on something smaller or delay buying a house until you have more money—and need only a smaller mortgage to make up the difference.

What You've Accomplished

- ✓ Calculated how much house you can afford
- ✓ Checked your credit report for inaccuracies
- ✓ Assembled your financial docs
- ✓ Learned how to choose a broker and lender
- ✓ Determined what mortgage is best for you
- ✓ Estimated closing and moving costs

Questions for Your Expert

If you still have questions about anything we've covered in this section, write them here and then go to www.learnvest.com/financiallyfearless for answers.

I still don't understand . . .

_____

_____

Where do I find . . .

_____

_____

What should I do about my . . .

_____

_____

Talk to an LV *Expert*

Examples:

In today's market, what's better: a fixed or ARM mortgage?

I still don't understand what goes into all of these closing costs. How do I estimate them?

Saving for Kids

As I'm sure the parents reading this book can agree, having kids is one of the most important, rewarding, and fulfilling experiences a person can have in life. It is also one of the most expensive. If you're planning for a baby in your future, whether that's a year away or a decade away, it's a wise idea to start putting some money aside. Once you have kids, money nearly evaporates, so it's never too soon to ask that timeless question . . .

How Much Will This Baby Cost Me?

I'm not going to sugarcoat it for you. The answer: a *lot*. The average middle-class family in the United States will spend about $234,900 raising a child from birth to the age of seventeen, according to a USDA report.[40] If you're in a higher income bracket, odds are you'll spend twice that.[41] And given you'll need full-time child care during the first years, which are usually the most costly (until they get to be college age, at least, but we'll get to that), it pays to start saving up as early as possible.

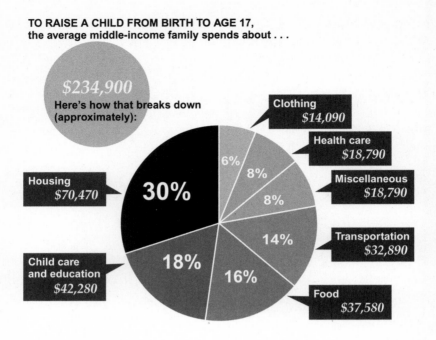

TO RAISE A CHILD FROM BIRTH TO AGE 17,
the average middle-income family spends about . . .

$234,900
Here's how that breaks down (approximately):

Clothing $14,090

Health care $18,790

Miscellaneous $18,790

Transportation $32,890

Food $37,580

Housing $70,470 — 30%

Child care and education $42,280

18%

16%

14%

8%

8%

6%

Opening an Account

The first thing to do is to start a baby-specific savings account. There will be a lot of competing baby expenses in the future, so the more you're able to direct to this goal now, the better. If you can put away just $200 a month and are five years away from having a baby, you'll have $12,000 by the time you have your baby. That could cover maternity leave (if your employer doesn't pay you for it) or a few months of day care when you return to work. Remember that this comes out of your 20 bucket, so how much you decide to squirrel away will depend on your other savings priorities.

While it's obviously ideal to start putting money in a baby fund years in advance, once the baby is on its way, that baby is coming, savings or no savings. The rest of this section will walk you through everything you need to know to budget for the new addition to your family—while keeping your baby-related costs as low as possible. Let's face it, you're not going to be sleeping much for a while once this expensive little angel arrives, and the last thing you need is to lie awake between feedings worrying about how the hell you're going to afford all the formula and diapers.

Maternity Leave and Paternity Leave

If you work, your employer probably has standard maternity and paternity leave policies that you should get to know before the big day. In the United States, paid maternity leave usually depends on your employer—and benefits can vary widely. If you work for a big company with good benefits, it's pretty standard to get at least six weeks of paid time off for maternity leave. However, if you work for a smaller employer or a company that does not have generous benefits, you can do what many women do: take a combo of sick leave, personal days, short-term disability, vacation, and unpaid family leave.

Thanks to 1993's Family and Medical Leave Act (FMLA), most new parents in the United States can leave their jobs for twelve weeks after a new baby without threat of being fired. That doesn't mean they're guaranteed any pay, though. I say most because if your company is small (under fifty employees) or you're not a full-time employee, you may not qualify in any case.

It's pretty embarrassing, actually, how bad parental leave benefits are in the United States. According to CNN, only about 12 percent of American workers get paid family leave, and close to half of American workers have no FMLA protection, meaning their jobs are vulnerable if they take time off to take care of a new baby.[42] We're one of very few countries without mandatory paid time off for new parents. Yes, we're hanging with Swaziland and Papua New Guinea. Meanwhile, Denmark gives couples *fifty-two weeks* of paid leave, of which two weeks are guaranteed to the father and eighteen to the mother and the rest distributed as the family deems appropriate.[43] (Pretty enticing, but then you'd have to live in *Denmark*, and do they have good BBQ there? They do not.)

Thank goodness some states are more progressive than the

federal government, though, and offer better maternity and pa-ternity leave than required by federal law (DC, Connecticut, New Jersey, and California, for example, are considered "top states for new dads" on account of their paternity leave policies).[44] As soon as you know you're going to have a baby, check your local laws and your company's policies. And no matter what your state man-dates or your company offers, start stockpiling vacation and sick days like they're water in a drought (check your work policy first to see how many days you can accumulate and roll over). Trust me, no matter how much time off you get, it's not going to feel like enough once the baby comes.

Also, keep in mind that while on unpaid leave, you won't be eligible to contribute to your 401(k) or flexible spending accounts (FSAs).

FEARLESS LESSON | *Questions to Ask HR About Maternity Leave*

- What is the most basic paid maternity leave plan available?

- What is the policy on short-term disability days? (Keep in mind that short-term disability should always cover your salary—or a portion of it—for a certain amount of time, which will vary by state.)

- How many unpaid family-leave days can I take for maternity leave?

In general, six weeks is the standard amount of time covered for preg-nancy, although you could be eligible for eight weeks or longer after a C-section birth or if you had any medical complications (God forbid). After receiving answers to the questions above (from your HR website or HR rep directly), you should be able to figure out how long you can take off after a normal birth and how much of that time would be unpaid.

Health Insurance

Employers are obligated to keep you on their health insurance plan while you're on maternity leave, but they *aren't* obligated to keep paying your health insurance costs in full. For instance, some companies will pay your premiums but ask you to reimburse them for the share that is no longer coming out of your paycheck. I recommend calling your benefits department and finding out what co-pays and medical expenses your employer will *not* cover, so you can budget accordingly.

FEARLESS LESSON   *Questions to Ask HR About Health Insurance*

- What will my health insurance plan cover in terms of prenatal doctor visits and delivery? (Be sure to check out benefits related to the exact type of delivery you are planning for—hospital, home, etc.). What will the co-pays be?
- Which pregnancy or baby-related products will be covered by my FSA account? Examples include breast pumps, lactation consultation, and Lamaze classes. Fertility treatments, pregnancy tests, and ovulation-predictor kits may be covered as well.

Also, determine to whose health insurance policy it is best to add your baby. If you have a spouse or partner, which health insurance plan is more cost-effective and offers sufficient coverage? If you will be adding the baby to yours, be sure to factor in the revised cost.

Child Care

Child-care costs vary widely, but the major variables are the type of care and where you live. Generally speaking, the more convenient the care (e.g., a live-in nanny), and the more urban your environment (e.g., Manhattan, L.A., Chicago), the more it will cost you.

Usually the most costly option is a full-time, live-in nanny or au pair. (An au pair, who is usually a young person that comes to the United States from a foreign country to live with you and do a certain number of hours of child care in exchange for room, board, and a weekly stipend, can be cheaper than a nanny.) If you can't afford a nanny—and let's be clear, most people can't—day care is a much cheaper option. Formal day-care centers are typically more expensive than those run out of a home. These days nanny sharing—that is, sharing the cost of a nanny with a few other parents—is becoming a popular option. Send out feelers via Facebook or ask around the playground or neighborhood to find other parents who might be interested in going in on one. Obviously the cheapest child care is having a family member look after your baby (though that often comes with its own costs, usually psychological ones). And of course, if you or your spouse decides to stay home with the baby, it'll cost whatever income is being lost.

Here's a chart with rough estimates of what these options cost. Look at the high end if you live in a major city and the low end if you live in a smaller town or rural setting.[45]

TYPE OF FULL-TIME CARE	NATIONAL AVERAGE MONTHLY COST
Family member staying at home	The cost of lost wages
Day care in someone's home	$400–$900
Day care at a center	$400–$1,200
Preschool (ages 2–5)	$400–$1,100
Au pair	$500–$1,400 (plus several thousand dollars in program and placement fees)
Nanny	$2,000–$3,000 (less if you share a nanny with another family!)

Now that you have a general idea of how much the different types of child care will cost you, the next step is to figure out whether it makes more financial sense to go back to work full-time, part-time, or forgo returning altogether. Since everyone's personal situation is different and all the variables make this too complicated to explore here, go to www.learnvest.com /financiallyfearless, where you can enter your income and child-care expenses and see how your potential new budget will shake out. If you prefer to do the math on your own, remember that in addition to child care, you may need to get help with cleaning and errands if you decide to work full-time.

FEARLESS TIP   *Name a Guardian*

Once baby arrives, you will need to name a legal guardian. This is a critical part of planning for your child's future, so be sure to consider not only how this person may raise your child in terms of values, but also how prepared he or she is *financially* to handle the added pressures of caring for a child.

Of course, expensive as they are, child-care costs for your baby or toddler are going to seem like pocket change down the line when it's time to start thinking about paying for (gulp!) college.

What You've Accomplished

✓ Opened a savings account for your future child costs

✓ Researched your maternity/paternity leave options

✓ Talked to HR about health insurance coverage

✓ Considered child-care options

✓ Started to think about a legal guardian

Questions for Your Expert

If you still have questions about anything we've covered in this section, write them here and then go to www.learnvest.com/financiallyfearless for answers.

I still don't understand . . .

_____

_____

Where do I find . . .

_____

_____

What should I do about my . . .

_____

_____

Talk to an

LV

Expert

Examples:

My company has really limited parental leave options. What do I need to do to make up for this?

Child-care costs in my area are extremely high. What options do I have to fit quality child care into my budget?

College Savings

(529 Plans, Coverdell, and More)

Maybe you have kids. Maybe you're thinking about having kids. Either way, a big issue on the minds of most parents or potential parents is how the hell they are going to afford their children's educations. I know, I know, paying for college seems like a one-way ticket to the poorhouse, especially now that some private colleges are charging more than $50,000 *a year*.[46] With tuition rising at a rate of up to 5 percent a year, often exceeding the rate of inflation (and experts predicting that a four-year degree from Harvard may cost half a million dollars by 2027),[47] how can anyone keep up? Part of the answer lies in college savings accounts, which provide a place to grow your money quickly and safely, so that by the time your children are applying to college, you'll be able to cover a significant portion of their expenses, if not all of them.

> **FEARLESS** LESSON   *Public vs. Private College*
>
> The average cost of tuition plus fees at a private college in 2012–2013 was $29,056. In-state tuition and fees at a public university: $8,655.[48] So is paying way more for a private college worth it? Maybe not. A researcher in one study suggested that "those who attend a regional public master's university might be getting 90 percent of the value of an education at an elite private for 20 percent of the cost."[49] Just something to keep in mind.
>
> However, as much as you would love to send your child, all expenses paid, to the school of their dreams, you should always pay down your debt and max out your retirement contributions **before** putting money toward your child's college account. Why? I'll repeat: your child can always apply for financial aid, loans, or grants, but there is no government assistance or loans for credit-card debt or for retirement.

College Savings Accounts in a Nutshell

Okay, so let's say you're free of debt, you're putting away 5 percent a month (or whatever your employer matches) for retirement, and you have some money left over to start a college savings account (on behalf of your children or future children, let me just say thank you). So how do these accounts work?

Essentially, college savings accounts are investment accounts that give you special tax benefits. These plans are pretty win-win for both the plan's owner (in this case, you) and its beneficiary (your child). As the owner, you will receive whatever state tax benefits are available for contributions (there are no federal tax benefits for such savings plans), while the beneficiary of your plan will get to use the funds.

It's important to note that these are **investment** accounts, not traditional savings accounts. This works in your favor, since you want your money to grow, and at a faster pace than 2 percent to 3 percent inflation. Think about it this way. The Consumer Price Index (a measure of inflation) rose only 1.7 percent in 2012 (after a 3 percent increase in 2011),[50] while college tuitions are rising at around 2 percent to 5 percent **a year.**[51] What this means is that if you tried saving up for your child's education in a traditional savings account, which as of August 2012 earned only 1 percent interest at the most, by the time your child was ready to go to college, your money would actually be worth *less* than when you put it in there! Again, as with other forms of investing, time is on your side: **the further in advance you save for college, the less you'll pay overall.** We love compounding interest.

You might be hoping that once your child gets within reach of college, you can fund his or her education with some free money thanks to grants and scholarships. Well, that would be nice, and I'm sure your child or future child is very deserving, but according to the College Board, grants pay for only about the same amount of tuition as loans do: an average of between $6,000 and $7,000 each in 2011–2012.[52]

In other words, if you don't have the savings, you and/or your kids may well need to take out student loans to bridge the gap. This is especially important as student loans have become an untenable burden for graduating students. (See page 144 for more on the student-loan crisis.) And it's not just the graduates themselves who are feeling the pain; middle-aged Americans are among the people struggling the most with student loans right now—because they took out loans beyond their means to finance their own kids' education. So if you are dead set on paying your kid's tuition, the solution is to start contributing to a college savings plan long before your child goes off to college—ideally before he or she has even mastered finger painting. Every dollar saved now is a dollar less you'll have to borrow in the future.

And as your child grows closer to college age, don't keep your head in the sand when it comes to talking about the costs ahead. Do sit down early and talk with your child about how taking sizable student loans will impact him or her financially post-college. Help your child make an educated decision about where to attend school with a sound understanding of what borrowing really means.

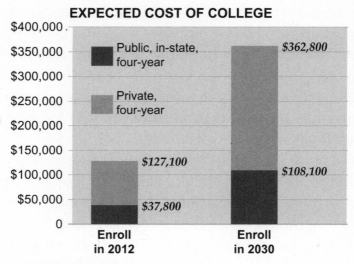

EXPECTED COST OF COLLEGE

Source: SavingforCollege.com

The Types of College Savings Accounts

There are three main kinds of college savings accounts you need to know about.

1. 529 College Savings Investment Plans[53]

A 529 savings plan is a type of investment account sponsored by individual states that allows you to save for your child's college education, tax and penalty free (as long as the funds are actually used for higher education expenses—that is, you don't divert them to pay for, say, your child's wedding or first apartment instead). **What to know:**

- It's available to you regardless of your income level.

- You can use the funds to pay for college-related expenses beyond tuition, including application fees, room and board, books, supplies, and equipment.

- If you use the money on anything else, you will be subject to heavy penalty fees of 10 percent on the earnings, plus you'll have to pay federal income taxes on the earnings. Some states might even add an additional 10 percent penalty for early withdrawal.

- It varies by state, but contribution limits are high, up to $360,000 total. But if you contribute more per year than the annual gift tax amount (which in 2013 is $14,000), your contribution may be treated as a gift and taxed if you don't meet the criteria for accelerated contributions. (A married couple can each contribute the annual gift tax amount per year, per beneficiary, so in 2013, $28,000 for a married couple.) Or you can contribute five years' worth of "gifts" in one year (in 2013, $70,000 for an individual or $140,000 for a married couple) and not incur a gift tax as long as you don't contribute anything else for the next four years. Anyone can contribute, so this goes for grandparents, too!

FEARLESS TIP *Gifting College*

Consider asking your families to make contributions to your children's 529 accounts instead of lots of traditional birthday and holiday gifts. Anyone can make a contribution, and this helps you sock away more resources for the big expenses that lie ahead. Wouldn't you rather Aunt Mildred put that $50 toward your kid's future instead of a new sweater or video game?

---

2. Prepaid Plans[54]

A prepaid plan is a type of 529 that may work for you if your child will attend an in-state public college. **What to know:**

- You'll get a locked-in price at the current average rate of tuition at state public schools, and if your child actually does go to an in-state public college, the plan will pay for tuition and required fees.

- If your child decides to attend a private or out-of-state college, this type of plan would typically pay the average in-state public college tuition, and you will be responsible for any difference in price.

- Most prepaid plans cover tuition only and can't be used to cover other expenses associated with school, such as room and board, without penalties.

Note: This is a big call to make early, so only do so if you're 100 percent sure that it's what both you *and* your child want.

3. Coverdell Plans[55]

A Coverdell account differs from a 529 investment plan in few ways. **What to know:**

- Only $2,000 a year total can be contributed, whether the full $2,000 comes from you or $1,000 comes from you and $1,000 from a grandparent.

- You can use the money in the plan for qualified primary and secondary education expenses (all the way from pre-K through high school).

- You can't contribute if your individual income is more than $110,000 or $220,000 if you file taxes jointly with your spouse.

Now that you know your options, here are the answers to a couple of questions we frequently get at LearnVest.

Top College Savings FAQs

1 What if I open an account and my child doesn't go to college? You're allowed to change the beneficiary of a 529, usually at least once a year, as long as it's to

another family member (the existing beneficiary's siblings, grandparents, first cousins, aunts and uncles)—or even to yourself (if you decide you want to use the funds for your own education, whether for a bachelor's or a higher degree).[56]

2 Will my 529 plan affect my child's chances for financial aid? Yes, but only slightly. If the 529 plan is owned by a parent (as opposed to, say, a grandparent), up to 5.6 percent of assets in that plan will be assessed for financial needs.

If you're ready to get started saving, go to www.learnvest.com/financiallyfearless to figure out how much *you* need to save each month to reach your college savings goal while still keeping your 50/20/30 budget intact.

Remember . . . with the right planning, you can get ahead when it comes to saving for college. But again, you should never put aside your retirement goals to save for college. This isn't being selfish; your child will feel the stress and burden, too, if you get to retirement age and don't have the financial means to support yourself!

What You've Accomplished

✓ Learned about the variety of payment options

✓ Opened a college savings account for your child(ren)

✓ Made a note to ask family and friends for college contributions in the future

Questions for Your Expert

If you still have questions about anything we've covered in this section, write them here and then go to www.learnvest.com/financiallyfearless for answers.

I still don't understand . . .

_____

_____

Talk to an

LV

Expert

Where do I find . . .

_____

_____

What should I do about my . . .

_____

_____

Examples:

I really want my child to go to a state school (my alma mater), but who knows what she'll want when the time comes! Is a prepaid plan still a good idea?

How much of my children's college educations can I afford to cover?

Helping Our Beloved Aging Parents

Great news! People are living longer! But, as our population enjoys increasingly longer golden years, many adult children are put in the position of becoming caretakers for their aging parents. And they are often blindsided by how insanely expensive elder care can be. (I mean, it's nuts.) It's estimated that ten million Americans have taken time off from work to care for their parents—resulting in a loss of $3 *trillion* in wages and retirement benefits.[57]

Your parents sacrificed a lot to raise you, so you may be thinking that it's your turn to repay the favor. Personally, I am obsessed with my mom, and I would do literally anything for her. So here are a few steps I recommend you take *now* to ensure that, should there come a time when you *do* have to support a parent, you'll be financially **prepared.**

Step 1. Research Their Situation

Get as much information as you can about not only your parents' wishes but also their medical, legal, and financial situation. The American Association of Retired Persons (AARP) recommends

you do this *before* an emergency so you have all necessary information at your fingertips. And if you live far away, introduce
yourself to your parents' friends and neighbors and get their
phone numbers and e-mail addresses the next time you visit.
This way you'll be able to contact them if there's ever a problem
and you need feet on the ground. Take advantage of the low-cost
and/or free resources out there. Start with the Department of
Health and Human Services' Eldercare Locator (eldercare.gov),
a tool that helps find local agencies that offer services like home
care, meals, and transportation.

Step 2. Make Sure They Have Insurance

Know the different types of insurance options for your parents,
including Medicare, Medicaid, Medigap, and long-term-care insurance.

- **Medicare** is the federal insurance program for
  Americans age sixty-five and older. Part A helps cover
  inpatient hospital care and skilled nursing facilities, but
  not long-term care; Part B pays for doctor services and
  outpatient care. The Medicare Rights Center, which
  works to ensure access to affordable health care for older
  adults, has an interactive site—Medicare Interactive—
  that provides personalized information and advice on
  Medicare.

- **Medicaid** is the joint federal-state program for low-
  income individuals. Income and resource requirements
  vary by state. According to AARP, it is possible in some
  states for individuals with high medical bills to "spend
  down" their income to become eligible for Medicaid
  benefits.

- **Medigap** is private insurance that helps fill gaps in
  Medicare coverage.

- **Long-term-care insurance** covers nursing homes, among other things. The earlier you buy this, the better: the premium goes up depending on your parents' health and age.

Step 3. Figure Out Who the Caregiver Will Be—and What to Do If It's You

It's not fun to think about, but whether it's due to disease, injury, or mental decline, there may come a time when your parents cannot—and should not—live on their own. Given that this is bound to be a very emotional and tough moment for all involved (and your parents may not be in a mental or physical state to make good decisions), I suggest that you investigate housing and care options and discuss them with your parents well in advance. A private geriatric care manager can help you understand and weigh your options. Also know that if you choose to have your parents come live with you, you may be eligible for a tax deduction by claiming them as dependents or for a tax credit that will allow you to deduct a portion of the cost of in-home care. Under the Family and Medical Leave Act, large employers are required to provide up to twelve weeks of unpaid leave with job protection for individuals caring for an ailing parent.

If you have siblings, you'll need to talk to them about your shared responsibilities. What role will each of you play in the family plan? And do you all know the state of your parents' estate documents? They should have a living will, a last will and/or living trust, a power of attorney (POA) for health care, and a health-care proxy named. We all love our parents, so it's critical to give back to them by having a solid game plan.

What You've Accomplished

✓ Talked to your parents about their financial situation

✓ Located contact info for local friends, neighbors, and others in case of emergency

✓ Looked into local support resources

✓ Checked your parents' insurance policies (specifically: health and long-term-care insurance)

✓ Researched caregiver options

✓ Consulted with other family members to establish a plan

✓ Confirmed that your parents have the appropriate estate docs in place (including a living will, power of attorney for health care, and health-care proxy)

Questions for Your Expert

If you still have questions about anything we've covered in this section, write them here and then go to www.learnvest.com/financiallyfearless for answers.

I still don't understand . . .

_____

_____

Where do I find . . .

_____

_____

What should I do about my . . .

_____

_____

Talk to an
LV
Expert

Examples:

My parents don't know where to find all of their financial info. How can I help them locate and access everything?

Caregiver costs are extremely high, and my parents don't have long-term-care insurance. What are our other options?

Major Purchases

(Trips, Homes, Cars, Starting a Business)

When I say that money doesn't have to get in the way of your living your richest life, I mean it. So far this 20 section has been all about putting away money for things the future you will *need*, **but this slice of the 20 section of the pie is about saving for the things the future you will want.** But how exactly do you put those high-price-tag dreams like a new car or a trip to Istanbul within reach? I recommend these three simple steps.

Step 1. Be Specific About What You Want

What *exactly* are you saving up for? Be as specific as possible, so you can be realistic about getting there. In other words, make it your "2013 Audi A6 fund" not your "car fund." The more specific you are, the more you'll visualize the reward and thus the more you'll be motivated to save.[58]

Step 2. Set Up Separate Accounts for Each Big-Ticket Item

If you anticipate reaching your goal in the next five years, keep your money in a high-yield savings account rather than taking the risk of investing these funds (even if banks are only paying 1 percent interest). Instead of keeping one massive stash of savings funds (which will make it all the more complicated to track your progress), see if your current bank offers subaccounts. That way, you'll have a separate account for everything (your "trip to Paris fund" will be separate from your "lake house fund"). If your current bank doesn't allow you to easily split your savings account, the LearnVest Money Center lets you set goals on your accounts.

> *Talk to an*
>
> LV
>
> *Expert*

If your goal will take far north of five years to achieve, consider putting your money in a brokerage account to help it grow faster.

Step 3. Automate

Not to sound like a broken record, but this is the perfect opportunity to automate. Simply set up a direct deposit and send a set percentage of your income straight to your specific goal accounts each month. Keep your savings account in a separate bank from where you have your checking. Save yourself the temptation of tapping into this until your savings bucket is full. Out of sight, out of mind! You won't miss what you don't see.

What You've Accomplished

✓ Put price tags on your specific goals

✓ Opened high-yield saving accounts or subaccounts

✓ Automated deposits into these saving accounts

Questions for Your Expert

If you still have questions about anything we've covered in this section, write them here and then go to www.learnvest.com/financiallyfearless for answers.

I still don't understand . . .

_____

_____

Where do I find . . .

_____

_____

What should I do about my . . .

_____

_____

Examples:

I have a lot of different major purchases I'm saving for. How do I prioritize these against my other goals?

How do I find out if my bank offers subaccounts?

I want to start a company. What do I do to save?

Talk to an

Lᴠ

Expert

Other Investments

This book isn't about getting rich; it's about getting control over your finances so you can live a richer life. It's about organizing your money, creating a detailed and balanced budget, and improving your financial habits so you can make smart money decisions on autopilot, without even having to think about it.

Lots of people think investing is about getting rich by picking winning stocks or trying to beat the market (which is virtually impossible), but in reality investing is about putting your money to work for you without your ever having to do the heavy lifting.

I don't know about you, but I *love* the idea that when I'm hanging out with friends or having a crazy day at work or sleeping like a baby—no matter where I am or what I'm doing—**my money is working for me.** I can sit back and know that I'm doing something right to maximize my dollars. In this section I'm going to show you how to get the big picture of your portfolio on track so you can make your money work even when you're not.

> **FEARLESS** LESSON *The Five-Year Rule*
>
> When you're deciding what money to invest, know what I call **the five-year rule.** This rule of thumb says that you should **only invest money that you won't need to use for at least five, maybe even seven or eight, years.** Why? Well, the market is known to be unpredictable, and you don't want to be in a position of *needing* to liquidate your funds in the middle of a dip (thereby taking a loss). Just something to always consider!

Investing Rules to Live By

Investing is complicated. It can be overwhelming. And there are countless people who have made it their full-time job to try to beat the market. But unless you have twenty-four hours a day to spend researching stocks and scrutinizing the market (and even that's no guarantee—according to a 2009 study, 70 percent of day traders lose money and 95 percent will fail in the first two years[59]), this is a fool's errand. Instead, you want to make smart, long-term investments that will stand up to ebbs and flows in the market and grow your nest egg over time.

The thing about investing, though, is that it's personal. Your circumstances and risk tolerance play a large role in determining the "right" investment decisions for you. It's critical to educate yourself, so you can make smart choices and think through what investment strategy is most suitable for *you*.

That said, there are some important investing principles that I believe a savvy investor needs to know.

1. Choose a Discount Broker—but Do Your Research First

There are two major categories of brokerage firms out there: **full service** and **discount.** Full-service firms will hold your hand through investment decisions—in exchange for very *steep* fees. So even if you're making a lot on your investments, the fees charged by full-service brokers will seriously slash your earnings. Unless you're working with millions, discount is typically the way to go. Discount firms charge as little as $5 to $15 per trade and don't come with the same hefty annual fees and commissions.

At the end of the day, **you can't control the market, but you** *can* **control the fees you pay.**

What to Look for in a Brokerage Firm

MINIMUM TO OPEN AN ACCOUNT. How much does the brokerage firm require you to invest in order to open an account there—$1,000? More? Can you meet that minimum?

ACCOUNT MINIMUM. Does the brokerage firm charge a fee if your balance falls below a certain amount?

COMMISSIONS. What are the charges for trades?

MAINTENANCE FEES. Is there an annual maintenance fee?

MANAGEMENT FEES. Are there ongoing management fees?

OTHER FEES. Any other cash you'll have to pony up?

SERVICES. What exactly does the broker offer? Make a phone call or check the website for a "What We Offer" or "Our Services" kind of heading—you'll probably find this kind of info there.

GOOD WEBSITE. You should be doing a lot of your account maintenance online, so it's important that you like the feel of the site. Is it easy to navigate? Can you easily figure out how to open an account? Can you quickly locate a way to contact customer service by phone?

Track your findings with the chart that follows and make a list of questions you'd like to ask the brokerage firm.

BROKERAGE NAME	MINIMUM TO OPEN	ACCOUNT MINIMUM	COMMISSIONS	MAINTENANCE FEES	MANAGEMENT FEES	OTHER FEES	SERVICES	GOOD WEBSITE?

2. Choose ETFs and Index Funds, Not Individual Stocks

ETFs (exchange-traded funds) and index funds contain a broad and varied assortment of stocks (which ensures that you're not making the risky move of putting all your eggs in one basket). Most ETFs and all index funds are meant to replicate an index (like the S&P 500). An ETF trades on an exchange, as the name suggests, and is bought and sold like a stock—at price per share. The benefit of both of these is that you get instant diversification— exposure to thousands of stocks, all for very low fees.

Mutual funds, which also contain an assortment of stocks (or bonds), can provide similar diversification, but because their assortments are handpicked by portfolio managers, they may leave you overly exposed to a handful of stocks or certain types of stocks. They are basically index funds with an active strategy. Because of this, you will pay additional fees for the fund manager's services. Due to diversification, mutual funds are inherently less risky than trying to handpick individual stocks, but I think your *best* bet is the ETF or index fund.

3. Assess Your Risk on a Goal-by-Goal Basis

In investment-speak, risk is the chance that you'll lose part of your investment. (You know what they say: greater risk, greater reward—but that's not always the case.) We'll get deeper into how to assess your risk profile in a minute, but before we do, note that your risk profile need not be consistent across all of your financial goals. If you hope to buy a house in ten years, you might be more conservative with the funds you're investing in toward that purchase than with those in your retirement account, which you may not need for thirty-plus years.

Simply put, the longer your time horizon for reaching a specific goal, the more risk you can afford to take on.

4. Diversify (and Try Alternatives)

As you diversify (i.e., invest in a wide range of things), think broadly. Beyond domestic versus international stocks, large-cap versus small-cap, you can consider purchasing alternatives— investments that typically go in the opposite direction as the overall market. This includes things like real estate investment trusts (REITs), commodities, natural resources, gold, oil, etc. You don't have to go to the nearest jewelry store and stock up on gold; there are actually ETF funds that dabble in alternatives. Before committing to alternatives as part of your investment game plan, take the time to assess the risk and decide whether it's something you're willing to take on.

5. Rebalance

As the market fluctuates, it's important to stick with your long-term strategy. Set calendar reminders to check your investment accounts on at least a quarterly basis, and when it appears you've gotten off balance from your long-term strategy, take the time to rebalance.

FEARLESS LESSON   *How Much Risk to Take On?*

Virtually all financial experts agree that **the younger you are, the more risk you can afford to take on (when it comes to investing, as with retirement saving, time is on your side).** But what does that mean for you, exactly? Here's another rule of thumb I recommend: the **rule of 120.** In order to get a sense of what percentage of your account to invest in stocks, take 120 and subtract your age. So if you're thirty-five, 85 percent of your portfolio would be invested in stocks or equities (the two terms are synonymous) and the rest in bonds.

But no matter how old you are, in general you should take on only as much risk as your personality can handle—and if you can't stomach the wild swings that might come with having a large percentage of your money in stocks, that might not be the best mix for you. You have to give some thought to how comfortable you are with the risk of losing money. How much could you lose without freaking out? Be honest. If you opened your 401(k) statement tomorrow and discovered that the balance had fallen by 15 percent, would you run for cover? If even a 5 percent loss would leave you panic stricken, you may need a more conservative approach than stocks, like bonds or money markets. Not sure exactly how high your risk tolerance is? We have a risk-assessment tool at www.learnvest.com/financially fearless.

Finding "the One"

So now you know why, and how much, you should be investing in ETF, index, or mutual funds. But that's only half the battle given that there are thousands and thousands of funds out there to choose from. And while you may have a money manager helping you out, you should never put your cash into anything you don't understand. You want to make sure you're asking the right questions, and it's definitely worth your while to do a little reading on your options before taking a monetary leap (though you can always talk to a professional if you're totally lost).

How to Research Funds[60]

Step 1. Go to Morningstar.com

One of the best places to start is Morningstar.com, which provides copious amounts of information on a variety of investment choices—so much info, in fact, that you can get a little bit lost in the numbers. The steps that follow will help guide you.

Step 2. Enter the Ticker Symbol for the Investment You'd Like to Research

The star ranking at the top merely indicates how the fund is doing compared to other funds in its category, so a low ranking here doesn't necessarily mean it's a bad choice overall. (A caveat: if it has only one star, that can be a red flag, so you want to poke around to see what the story is.)

Step 3. Check the Fund's Expenses

That percentage refers to how much it costs on an annual basis for every dollar you have in that fund relative to that fund's assets. Anything under 1 percent is considered low, but the closer the number is to 0 percent, the better. Also check out the turnover rate, which reflects how much of the fund is bought or sold in a year. The lower the turnover, the better (high turnover = higher fees). A turnover of 50 percent or less is considered low.

Step 4. Look at the Fund's Diversification

Depending on your goals, it may be wise to invest in funds that are a diversified mix of stocks, bonds, and other types of funds. You can view the fund's "Top Holdings" and "Top Sectors" to see how its money is allocated and how diverse its holdings are.

Step 5. Check What the Fund's Minimum (i.e., the Minimum Investment Required to Get into the Fund) Is

This doesn't necessarily indicate a good or a bad investment, but if you don't have enough money to meet the fund's minimum, you can move on.

Step 6. See What the Fund's Load (i.e., How Much It Costs to Buy or Sell This Fund) Is

I recommend that you always opt for no-load funds, which charge no fee for buying into them—that's a good thing since it means you keep more of your money.

Step 7. Find Out How Much Cash Is in the Fund by Looking at Its "Asset Allocation"

If you see a fund with a significant amount in cash (upwards of 10 percent), it could mean that the fund's manager is trying to time the market. (In other words, the manager is holding some of the fund's money in cash and trying to pounce on good deals. I've seen very few managers who are any good at this and this strategy could lose serious money.)

Step 8. See Where the Fund Falls on Morningstar's Tic-Tac-Toe "Style Map"

This will give you some indication of whether the fund tends to invest in larger or smaller companies and whether it focuses on growth companies or value companies (which represent different types of risk). You want a mix of all of these things in your portfolio, so make sure that all of your investments don't fall into just one square.

Step 9. Investigate the Present Investments

Contrary to popular belief, the way a fund did last year or the year before doesn't necessarily predict its performance in the future. It's most important to make sure you agree with what that fund is invested in *now* and how it fits into your portfolio.

What You've Accomplished

- ✓ Selected a discount broker that meets your needs
- ✓ Assessed your risk profile online
- ✓ Learned the rule of 120 to determine a possible allocation
- ✓ Figured out how to research an investment

Questions for Your Expert

If you still have questions about anything we've covered in this section, write them here and then go to www.learnvest.com/financiallyfearless for answers.

I still don't understand . . .

_____

_____

Talk to an

LV

Expert

Where do I find . . .

_____

_____

What should I do about my . . .

_____

_____

Examples:

If I'm retiring in ten years, how should I allocate my portfolio?

I'm comfortable taking on a lot of risk but may need the funds in less than five years. Can I still invest?

the

30

—

YOUR LIFESTYLE

Congratulations. In completing those last two sections, you've just taken a seriously big step in getting your finances under control. Now that you've gotten the boring essentials out of the way *and* begun to lay a solid foundation for your future, it's time to talk about the fun stuff: lifestyle. At LearnVest, we macro-budget the 50 and the 20. Then, once that's under control, whatever is left over (up to 30 percent of your take-home pay) is yours to play with. You may not be able to have it all (no one can, at least not all the time!), but I promise that once you have your 50/20/30 plan in place, you'll be able to have a whole lot more of the things that make your life truly rich.

Just because we're talking about fun stuff doesn't mean there aren't some major lessons to be learned here. The big takeaways?

1. Spending Is Okay

We have to spend to live; it's a legitimate part of our lives. At the end of the day, we have to buy clothes so we can look the part at work. We have to exercise so we can invest in our health (our most valuable asset). We have to eat well to give us energy and nutrition. The list goes on, and it all leads to the bottom line. It's not the spending that's a problem. **It's the misguided spending that can be dangerous.**

We've all worked really hard and have earned the right to spend—a little—on the things we're passionate about. So let's get rid of the guilt and focus on spending *smarter,* on spending on the things that you value. Which brings me to my second point.

2. Learn to Spend Where It Counts

The 30 is a limited amount, which means it's critical to spend it where you notice it—*not* on magazines you throw away at the end of the month or premium cable when you never turn on the TV. Every dollar should go toward something you notice. After all, there are a million things pulling you all over the place, and if you don't make smart decisions, you'll end up blowing all your cash on things that you don't really care about instead of the things that truly add value to your life.

I have a simple equation I use when I'm deciding what to spend my 30 on that runs through my head every day. I call it "cost per happy." Your cost per happy is simply how much something costs divided by how happy it makes you. (I'll show you exactly how to calculate this in the next section.) For me, one of the things that has the lowest cost per happy is flowers. Let me explain. Every three months, I buy a new orchid. I go to my favorite shop in the flower district and pick out two tall white ones in a lovely glass container surrounded by moss. I pay $30 for the plants (a negotiated price, since I'm a regular). Once I've brought it safely home, it immediately goes on display in my living room.

Each time I walk by it, it makes me smile. Though I'm no green thumb, these orchids have a life span of three and a half months. So that's around 105 days of orchid-induced happiness. All for the price of $30, or less than thirty cents per day.

Now let's be clear: There will be moments when you have to put your 30 toward things you'd rather not, like an expensive trip to a friend's wedding or yet another happy hour for work. I won't pretend that you'll be able to avoid less-than-ideal spending altogether, but you can make great strides in learning to spend where you care. This is an individual challenge, but also a challenge you face as you merge your finances with your partner's. It's up to both of you to get in sync so you spend in the same direction and allow your dollars to bring you the maximum amount of happiness.

Money = Happiness?

Speaking of happiness, I don't believe that it can be bought. But I *do* believe that if you spend on the things you value, you can bring greater satisfaction to your life in a variety of important ways. What makes you happy is incredibly personal. For me, silly, simple flowers do it. For my husband, it's a delicious dinner out with friends. For one friend, it's a spin class after a tough week. For another, it's tennis lessons for her kids. What do you spend on that brings joy to your life?

This is the moment to think hard about what you **savor** the most when it comes to money. Since spending is a given, would you rather spend on an experience you won't enjoy, a new outfit you won't wear, a new gadget that will gather dust, or on the things you *value, notice, and care about*? **That's the exercise we all should master.** In this chapter, we're going to help you get at the heart of who you are when it comes to money and, in turn, how you choose to spend it.

FEARLESS LESSON   *Can You Buy Happiness?*

I'm sure we've all had the thought that we would just be so much happier if we made a bit more money. Yet researchers at Princeton say that 85 percent of Americans report feeling happy each day, regardless of their incomes.[1] In fact, they found that **after you start making more than $75,000 per year, the mood-elevating effects of a higher paycheck taper off** *completely.* The moral? Money alone can't buy happiness, especially once you've crossed the $75K mark. But what *can* make you happier is using that money wisely and in ways that improve your quality of life.

Calculating Your Cost per Happy

Your wallet is being pulled in a thousand different directions by just about everyone in your life—your significant other, your children, your friends. But the whole point of a financial plan is getting to use *your* money to follow *your* dreams. If your 30—your spare money, so to speak—is being eaten up by unused Netflix subscriptions and dusty gym membership cards, you're squandering an opportunity for joy.

What are we going to do about it? I want you to put *every single expense* through the cost-per-happy test. As you zero in on a balanced budget, know that small changes go a long way. If you traded one daily $5 expense that doesn't bring any happy to your life and instead invested it, in twenty years it could be worth over $69,000!

Let's do a test run.

Step 1

Think of an expense you've had in the past month.

Name your expense:

How much did it cost? $

Step 2

Ask yourself how happy it made you (on a scale of one to ten, one being "I could live without it" and ten being "It made me the happiest person in the world").

Write your happiness number here:

LESS THAN FIVE? It's time to say good-bye to this expense for good. It's simply not worth your money or time (after all, time is money). Check out tips for cutting this expense later on.

MORE THAN FIVE? This is clearly something you value, so move along to step 3 and see just how much.

Step 3

Ask yourself how long it made you happy for. Length of time can include the excitement of anticipation, like the giddiness you feel before a big trip, as well as the high of having done something great, like the satisfaction you feel after seeing your team win the big game from right behind home plate. Ultimately, we want to discover your cost per happy hour, so whatever the time, write it as an expression of an hour!

How many hours of happiness did you get from the expense?

Step 4

Take the cost of this expense (from step 1) and divide it by the number from step 3 to find your cost per happy for this expense!

$$\frac{\textbf{how much it cost}}{\substack{\textbf{how many hours of}\\\textbf{happiness it brought you}}} = \textbf{cost per happy}$$

There's no be-all and end-all cutoff for the actual number here, but this is a ridiculously easy way to compare your relative expenses. Deciding whether to go out for drinks with friends or go get a massage? Compare their cost per happy and the decision will be made for you.

You should never feel guilty about living your richest life. You've earned it, so enjoy it. And better yet, use this test to figure out what can bring you the most joy for a dollar.

Got it? Time to put this cost-per-happy process into action. Run the numbers for a range of lifestyle expenses (think of examples from your Money Center folders: restaurants/bars, travel, home, pets, entertainment, etc.). We've created a chart to stream-line things and given you some real-life examples.

COST PER HAPPY

EXPENSE	COST	RATING (on a scale of 1 to 10)	HOW MANY HOURS DID IT MAKE YOU HAPPY FOR?	COST PER HAPPY HOUR
Plane ticket for week-end beach getaway	$300	7	48 hours—all weekend long	$6.25
Dinner with friends	$50	8	2 hours	$25
Latest issue of Bon Appétit	$5	5	1/2 hour	$10

Your Spending Priorities

The calculation you've just learned will help you make the smartest decisions with every extra dollar that comes your way (which is the promise of a good financial plan). Now that you've mastered it, let's think more broadly about your spending priorities and how to maximize your cost per happy. Below are fifteen lifestyle categories that require money. Categorize them as high, medium, or low priorities (and no, they cannot all be high). Cross off the ones you don't care about, then rank those that remain. Be brutally honest! Remember, this is just for you.

- ☐ Beauty (hair, makeup, nails)
- ☐ Books and magazines
- ☐ Car
- ☐ Charity
- ☐ Eating out (Starbucks counts!)
- ☐ Entertainment (cable, concerts, movies)
- ☐ Exercise and sports (gym membership)
- ☐ Fashion (shopping for clothes)
- ☐ Gifts for others
- ☐ Hobbies (photography, scrapbooking, music, etc.)
- ☐ Home improvement (including decor and landscaping)
- ☐ Parenting (babysitters, allowance, kids' activities)
- ☐ Pets
- ☐ Technology (the latest iPad, other gadgets)
- ☐ Travel

HIGH	
MEDIUM	
LOW	

Study your numbers. You now see pretty clearly where your priorities are. What's important is to get a good sense of what you care about—whether it's having a second home or taking care of your kids or focusing on fashion and beauty—because *these* are the places you should be spending your 30.

Based on that exercise, fill out the following chart. On the left, list your top five priorities in order. On the right, list the last major purchase you've made in that priority category:

TOP FIVE PRIORITIES	LAST PURCHASE YOU MADE	PRICE YOU PAID
1.		
2.		
3.		
4.		
5.		

Now let's do the same for the opposite end of the spectrum:

BOTTOM FIVE PRIORITIES	LAST PURCHASE YOU MADE	PRICE YOU PAID
1.		
2.		
3.		
4.		
5.		

Take a step back. Here are the big questions: Have you put your money where your priorities are? How much money are you throwing away on things that are *not* top priorities? If your answer is "too much," don't worry. I'll give you a game plan for readjusting now.

Now that you've planned the 50 and 20 parts of your budget, they should be pretty automatic. Your housing costs are consistent from month to month. You have automatic deposits into your 401(k). That's all pretty fixed. But this 30 can be like the Wild West—anything can happen with those dollars, and planning is the best tip I can give you to make sure you don't end up losing out on a chance to maximize each and every one.

There's another hidden danger in the 30: this is the part of your budget your friends will try to derail. I always joke that your friends don't call you up and invite you to a "let's save for retirement party." No, they call you up and invite you to spend: on dinner, on vacations, on workout classes, on weddings. You need to be thoughtful with this 30 part of your budget so you ensure that it goes **where you want,** not where your friends or anyone else wants. In the next section I'm going to let you in on some amazingly simple money hacks to help you keep your spending in line with your priorities—*and* your budget.

Money Hacks

You now have the framework in place to be extra smart about your 30 percent, so let's get even smarter, one folder at a time. Here are the best tips—from our users, our LearnVest Program experts, and me—that will help you transform your spending habits and keep you on track.

 **General**

Tip 1   **Implement the PERK system.** Try sitting down and reviewing all your expenses in each category to determine which costs can be **Postponed** until a later date, **Eliminated** from your budget, or **Reduced** going forward and which expenses you absolutely have to **Keep** (hence the acronym PERK²).

Tip 2   **Lower recurring bills.** Go to LowerMyBills.com to see if you can lower your recurring bills, like cable and cell phone. Bear in mind you can contact these companies directly to negotiate and make sure you have the most efficient plan for your needs.

These two tips can work for pretty much any bill or expense. Now let's get a little more granular and look at more money hacks, specific to each spending category.

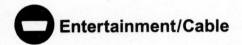 **Entertainment/Cable**

Tip 1   **Pay per view.** The average American cable subscriber spends $900 a year on the service.[3] But how many of us actually watch all those channels we're shelling out the money for? If you currently pay for premium cable service, test whether you really use or need it by calling your provider and putting the service on "vacation mode." After a month of doing without five different MTVs and seventeen different "on demand" channels, you can decide whether to restore or ditch the extra service. My guess is that instead of getting every channel imaginable, you'll be fine if you swap out traditional cable for Hulu Plus or Netflix, which are (at the time of writing) only about $8 a month and both offer on-demand TV and movies.

You could also consider a set-top box, such as Apple TV or ROKU, for under $100, which allows you to stream a variety of digital content (TV shows, movies, etc.) via the Internet.

Tip 2   **Never pay for music.** If you have some favorite artists or go through cycles of mild obsession with certain albums, then use a free service like Pandora or Spotify. It will cost you only if you really hate the commercials. Not only will these

services let you listen to the exact songs you want
to hear, but they will also introduce you to new
music you never knew you loved.

● Personal Care

Tip 1 **Calculate value.** Each year, American women
aged thirty to forty-nine spend an average of
approximately $1,200 on cosmetics alone.[4] That's
$12,000 over a decade, enough to buy a car! And
it's not just women: the industry sold $1.5 *billion*
worth of men's grooming products in 2010.[5] I'm
not saying to cut good-quality beauty products out
of your life (although I do recommend checking
out generic brands to save); I'm just suggesting you
pay attention to value, which takes into account
not just price but also the number of times you'll
actually use the item. To figure out your cost per
use, simply divide the cost of the item by the
number of times you use it. This is an equation
I keep in my head every time I shop.

Tip 2 **Space out treatments.** Again, if trips to the
hairdresser are something you care about, I'm
not here to tell you it's time to break up with your
stylist. But how about spacing things out? Instead
of reading this tip now and forgetting to actually
take action, head straight for your calendar and
book your next (spaced-out) appointments *now*.

⊖ Restaurants and Bars

Tip 1   **Utilize rewards.** There are all sorts of companies that will reward you for dining out, so make sure to take advantage. For example, making a reservation on OpenTable usually earns you one hundred points—let these add up and cash them in for a check that you can use at any OpenTable restaurant. It's pretty nice to get a discount just for making a reservation!

Tip 2   **Entertain at home.** Next time you're running out to meet a friend at a restaurant or a bar, remember that grabbing food or drinks at home can have enormous cost savings (not to mention convenience). The average U.S. diner spends over $450 per month on eating out (and that doesn't include drinks).[6] So skip the reservation and pick up a bottle of wine and snacks instead. Added bonus: you won't be rushed to give up seats as soon as you pay the bill!

⊖ Shopping

Tip 1   **Create a waiting period.** Instituting a waiting period before making a purchase can actually change your brain chemistry: if you take a break from an item for just two days, you'll be one third less likely to buy it.[7] Worried you'll forget what you wanted? I make a list of my wants on my phone. Sometimes I buy them. Sometimes they become gifts for my birthday. Oftentimes, I decide I don't really want 'em! Or, Pinterest.com lets you pin any photo on the Web to a virtual bulletin board for safekeeping until you can sleep on whether this item is truly a "need."

Tip 2   **Be savvy about marketing tricks.** Do you really like that bathing suit, or do you just like the fact that it costs $75 instead of its usual $150? Often, the "discount" may just be a marketing ploy. Research from the new field of neuromarketing reported in the *New York Times* has shown that if you have two similar items on a page, one selling for $200 and the other for $250, most people will choose the cheaper item. But add a third item at a higher price point, like $300, and now the same customer will buy the $250 item.[8] Sites often add high-price items they're unlikely to sell, seducing you into buying up. In other words, beware of the midrange buy.

 Gifts

Tip 1   **Stick to a budget.** Never embark on a gift excursion without a budget beforehand. This is especially true around the holidays. If you go shopping with an itemized list and a budget for each individual gift, it will make it far easier to resist temptations and stick to your limits.

Tip 2   **Know these quirky gift card finds.** While gift cards may seem like a cop-out, they are popular for a reason. Especially handy is the Tango card, a flexible gift card that can be used at many retailers (such as Amazon, Target, and Zappos), put toward several charities (including Habitat for Humanity and the National Park Foundation), or even redeemed for cash. You can also buy gift cards for less than face value at sites like GiftCardGranny .com, where you can maximize those budgeted dollars.

Tip 3   **Recognize that more generous gifts are not always better.** When you give a gift, it often makes the recipient feel the need to return the kindness. Though you have the purest intentions, you can imagine that giving a fancy gift to a friend who is struggling to make ends meet may actually lead to stress. A modest but thoughtful gift is more likely to make everyone happier than an overly extravagant one.

 **Home**

Tip   **Time your shopping.** Like fashion, furniture has its seasons. Office furniture like desks and bookshelves tend to be cheaper in January, while October is the best time for dining room furniture. Patio furniture usually goes on sale at the end of the summer. Bedroom furniture is a perennial need, so it doesn't have a predictable sales pattern . . . but mattresses and box springs tend to go on sale in May and again in the fall. Also, keep in mind regular holidays such as Independence Day, Labor Day, and Memorial Day, when department stores have major sales. Items like bed frames and coffee tables can easily last you a decade. Treat these purchases as big investments, buy slowly, and make sure that these are a fairly timeless style that you won't find repulsive ten years down the road.

What to Buy When

January

Winter boots, clothing, and coats; suits; perfume; home furnishings; calendar; carpets and flooring; big appliances; linens and bedding; holiday supplies; office furniture; video

February

Winter boots, clothing, and coats; perfume; homes; home renovations; bicycles; cameras; home entertainment systems; video games; chocolates and candy

March

Sweaters and cashmere; china and flatware; air conditioners; gas grills; gardening tools; frozen food

April

Sweaters and cashmere; sneakers; vacuum cleaners; snow blowers; office furniture; cruises; electronics

May

Vacuum cleaners; cookware; refrigerators; big appliances; grilling supplies; small kitchen appliances; party supplies; electronics; mattresses and box springs

June

Men's suits; tools; cookware; paint; butter; champagne and sparkling wine; gym memberships

July

Suits; furniture; big appliances; paint; butter

August

Flip-flops; school supplies; trees, shrubs, plants; lawn mowers and swing sets; computers; MP3 players

September

China and flatware; wine; computers; jeans; MP3 players; cars; holiday airfare

October

Jeans; swimsuits; big appliances; dining room furniture; mattresses and box springs; air conditioners; gas grills; school supplies; toys; cars; health insurance

November

Wedding dresses; swimsuits; cookware; Christmas trees; frozen turkeys; toys; electronics

December

Wedding dresses; televisions; pools; small kitchen appliances; champagne and sparkling wine; frozen meat

 **Travel**

Tip 1 **Shop on Tuesday mornings for airfare.** Fare sales are often launched on Monday nights, so other airlines have matched these prices by Tuesday morning. When in doubt as to whether you should wait another week in case a better deal pops up, booking earlier is safer. If you wait, fares could go up *or* down, and usually fares go up by more than they go down (read: going down $50 versus going up by $300). Only bide your time if your flight isn't too full and you know the price is a lot higher than it should be.

Tip 2 **Be quick on your feet (and with your mouse).** Travel sites like Jetsetter, Tablet Hotels, and Vacationist let you access luxury, vetted hotels at great rates. If you have enough saved for an impromptu vacation, these should be your first stops for research. If you sign up for their e-mail lists, they'll give you a heads-up about upcoming sales so you know when to pounce.

Kayak's "Hacker" tool can help you find two separate one-way flights to make a round trip for less. Kayak also offers a fare chart so you can see trends in the ticket prices, and Bing has created a price-predictor tool to help you guess if fares are going up or down.

Some airlines promote one-hour sales on Facebook or Twitter only, so follow an airline for the best deals.

And instead of a pricey hotel or resort, consider renting a house or apartment through Airbnb. If staying in a stranger's house doesn't creep you out (and it shouldn't—a lot of the listings on Airbnb are second homes that just sit empty most of the time), this is a great way to get cozy, roomy accommodations for a fraction of the price. It's also great for families in need of multiple rooms!

Tip 3 **Decline car rental insurance.** Car rentals are full of hidden fees: collision damage waiver fees, airport surcharges, fuel charges, mileage fees, taxes, additional-driver fees, underage-driver fees, out-of-state charges, and equipment-rental fees for car seats or ski racks. Some of these may be unavoidable, but there's one fee you don't need to opt for: rental insurance. The clerk might try to press this on you, but in some states you likely already have enough coverage through your own car insurance and/or credit-card company—so do some research when you book your car and show up to the counter knowing what you need and what you don't.

FEARLESS TIP *Travel Rewards*

There are dozens of credit cards with great travel rewards out there, but not many that have **zero foreign transaction fees.** If you anticipate doing a lot of travel, be on the lookout for this perk. It may not be your day-to-day card, but make sure you have one for all international travel.

 **Charity**

Tip 1 **Donate to causes you LOVE.**[9] This section is all about spending on the things that really matter to **you,** and that rule goes for charity as well. Go to CharityNavigator.org and GiveWell.org to seek

out charities and pick the cause that means the most to you. Look for organizations that match your monthly pledges (such as Modest Needs) and see if your company has a matching program for charitable donations (many do).

Tip 2   **Combine charitable giving with gift giving.** There are great products right now, like the accessories from Feed Projects (www.feedprojects.com) and Toms (www.toms.com), that will let you buy friends stylish presents that have a deductible or charity component.

Tip 3   **Take your deduction.** You'll only get a tax deduction on charitable gifts if you itemize your deductions on your tax return. This only makes sense for people whose deductions would be greater than the standard amount, a category that can include property owners, business owners, and people with numerous medical expenses, but if this is you, be sure to list all charitable donations. If you're not sure whether it makes sense for you to itemize, consult an accountant or a tax service such as TurboTax.

⊖ Electronics

Tip 1   **Trade in.** Exchange programs—like the popular Trade & Save Program from Radio Shack—let you trade in old electronics purchased from any store in exchange for a gift card. In general, steer clear of programs with a participation fee, which will eat into your profits.

Tip 2   **Buy refurbished products.** Refurbished products are a great way to save money. They usually come with a warranty and include new parts and accessories. For example, refurbished Apple Store items go through a rigorous testing process and are backed by a one-year warranty.

 **Health**

Tip 1   **Negotiate gym membership.** Maybe you've never realized gym memberships are negotiable, or maybe you've been too shy to ask. No longer! The best time to negotiate is in January, when gym promotions abound. Scout out gyms in your area and ask about discounts. Don't be afraid to do some serious detective work: search online to see what people are paying for gyms in your area and ask around. Find the lowest going rate and ask your gym of choice to match that rate for you. (If you convince the gym you're interested in to simply drop its joining fee, you could save as much as $50 to $200!) As with all negotiations, if they can't give you what you're looking for (a lower rate), see what else they can throw in. Free personal training sessions? A gym bag? A couple of yoga classes?

Tip 2   **Leverage and save.** You may already be entitled to gym deals you're not even aware of. Some **health-care plans** provide discounts or reimbursements on gym memberships, so research yours. An example: Blue Cross Blue Shield's Care First provides up to 60 percent off membership fees. You could save as much as $360 per year if you usually pay $50 per month.

Exercise Apps to Try

If you find that you aren't using your gym membership (you know who you are) or recognize that you could do without it, cancel it immediately and find an alternative that works for you. There are countless free exercise apps out there that can keep you motivated outside the gym. My favorites? MapMyRun.com helps you find running routes, and its iPhone app tracks calorie usage and logs workouts. Nike Training Club provides more than eighty-five instructor-narrated fitness routines. It tracks your progress, allows you to create playlists, and has video demos for each move. Both are 100 percent free.

Meetup.com is also a great way to find groups of people into pretty much every athletic activity under the sun—from running to hiking to Zumba—and participation is almost always free.

 Kids

Tip 1   **Look into sharing sitters.** Nanny shares began in the 1980s, when families became dependent on dual incomes and started looking for alternative child-care options. Today they've gained in popularity since so many families have been unable to employ full-time nannies postrecession.

Co-op day cares are also booming, because they provide both community and steep discounts. Check www.preschools.coop to learn more. To start one of your own, you could always reach out to other parents in your area via e-mail or Facebook, or simply ask around on the playground.

Tip 2   **Avoid name brands.** There's no shame in clothing your kid in the knockoff version of some popular brand; most likely it came off the exact same assembly line as the "real" (read: overpriced) version. Remember, they grow up fast!

What You've Accomplished

- ✓ Linked your accounts to LearnVest so you know your spending patterns

- ✓ Calculated your 30 (30 percent of your take-home pay)

- ✓ Determined your "cost per happy" on at least five expenses

- ✓ Ordered your spending priorities

- ✓ Read up on the best money hacks to maximize your spending power

Questions for Your Expert

If you still have questions about anything we've covered in this section, write them here and then go to www.learnvest.com/financiallyfearless for answers.

I still don't understand . . .

_____

_____

Talk to an

LV

Expert

Where do I find . . .

_____

_____

What should I do about my . . .

_____

_____

Examples:

It looks like my priorities don't match up with how I'm spending, but a lot of my expenses here don't feel optional. How do I follow through with tough cuts?

I haven't tracked my spending before. What's the best way to figure out my spending history?

First, this is real life. Tons of crazy stuff can happen that we don't like. You bought this book because you want to put your money worries to rest. If you've worked your way to this point, you should find yourself with a game plan for everything within your power: spending on essentials, saving for the future, and maximizing what's left over to live the richest possible life. Now that you have your 50/20/30 plan all mapped out, it's time to take the next step and troubleshoot that plan; in other words, protect yourself from those things that are *outside* your control, like other people, your own refuse-to-die bad habits, and plain old bad luck.

Let's face it: shit happens. We all wish it wouldn't, but it does. Maybe our car breaks down. We break a bone. We get fired (from a job we hated anyway!). Our partner leaves us. A hurricane knocks down our home. (Sandy, anyone?) None of these things are fun. In fact, they just plain suck. But there *is* a way to make them merely miserable rather than both miserable and financially catastrophic. It's *my* job to tell you how!

This is the section where we play the worst-case-scenario game to think through the conceivable threats to your financial well-being and then find ways to protect you from them. Better to tackle these fears for a couple of hours now than to get blindsided down the road!

First we'll talk about insurance that protects you from the lousy side of life: things like tornadoes and medical emergencies. Then we'll look at how to protect yourself from problems you may run into with other people, like divorces and money-toxic friends. Finally we'll discuss ways to rid yourself of your lingering bad habits (don't feel bad; we all have them) so you can protect yourself from *you*.

PROTECT
YOURSELF

from

LIFE

Listen, I know that *insurance* is the most boring word in the English language. There's a reason why a recent study found that 6 percent of Americans would rather eat bugs than shop for insurance.[1] Fact. While it's certainly not as exciting as saving for your safari vacation to Cape Town, it *matters*. It is the foundation of a solid plan, and it could save your financial life.

To make sure you recognize the stakes, and to keep us all from falling asleep, we're going to liven up this chapter with plenty of stories from people just like you who learned the value of a shield—some who were able to use one to fend off tragedy and others who were unprotected and learned a tough lesson they can now share with you so **you don't have to learn first-hand.**

Note that there are many insurance options out there and not everyone needs every single kind. However, I do recommend that *everyone who is eligible* have the following, no matter what:

☐ **Health insurance**
   See page 237.

☐ **Renter's or homeowner's insurance**
   See pages 243 or 245.

Beyond that, answer these questions to determine which additional types of insurance you need to look into. Then feel free to jump ahead to just those sections that apply to you.

☐ Do you own a car or borrow one regularly?
You need **auto insurance** *(see page 251).*

☐ Does anyone depend on your income (significant other, children, etc.)?
You need **life insurance** *(see page 254).*

☐ Would you struggle financially if you were injured and no longer able to work?
You need **disability insurance** *(see page 248).*

☐ Would nursing-home costs crush your finances?
You need **long-term-care insurance** *(see page 259).*

☐ Do you have substantial assets?
You need **umbrella insurance** *(see page 261).*

Talk to an LV *Expert*

Note that there's insurance for just about everything. **Generally,** things like business liability insurance (hello, private-practice doctor!), pet insurance, or trip insurance are not worthwhile, but if you think they might be for you, it's best to talk to an expert.

Finally, remember that it's not enough to simply *have* the insurance; I believe it's critical to also have your documents in order so you don't have to go searching for them during what will probably be a stressful time. So once you've covered insurance, be sure to go to Docs in a Row on page 263.

FEARLESS TIP *Buyer Beware*

Why does *insurance* provoke such an "ughhhhh, anything but that!" reaction? I think it's a combination of the boring factor and the ick factor. In the past, some insurance dealers took advantage of people. They didn't necessarily earn the used-car-salesmen rep, but there was some sleaziness. While insurance is now a more closely regulated industry, you still need to be extra careful to do your homework and make sure you're getting the coverage that's best for you (and not for the broker's commission).

How to Buy Insurance

As you determine what types of insurance you need to purchase or which of your existing insurance policies you need to adjust, here are my recommended must-know steps to take:

Step 1. Check to See If Your Employer Has a Plan

Your employer may offer more types of insurance than you know—some of which are automatic and some that you have to opt into. The upside of getting coverage through work is that it's often easier and more affordable than finding it independently. You'll have access to lower group rates and can have the monthly premium taken right out of your paycheck. However, if you leave your job, you may have a gap in coverage while waiting for a policy at your new job to kick in or while you secure a new policy.

When evaluating a policy through your employer, check to see if it's portable—meaning that it will follow you even if you leave your current job.

FEARLESS LESSON *Don't Miss Open Enrollment*

Find out the date for open enrollment at your company, and mark it on your calendar as a recurring event. Health insurance providers in particular are notorious for changing their benefits and co-pays from year to year, so don't ever let the opportunity to evaluate your insurance plans pass you by!

Step 2. Find an Agent

If your employer doesn't offer a suitable plan or a plan at all, you have two options for working with an agent:

Go local. Ask for referrals from friends, family members, or colleagues or get a list of agents through your state's insurance agency.

1. Any agent you choose should be licensed to sell insurance and certified, whether that's as a Chartered Financial Consultant (ChFC), Certified Financial Planner™ (CFP®), or Financial Services Specialist (FSS), or in their insurance specialty, such as a Chartered Life Underwriter (CLU) or Life Underwriter Training Council Fellow (LUTCF) for life insurance.

2. You should look for an independent agent with an insurance brokerage firm who can recommend policies from a wide range of companies to find the best value for your particular situation. **Don't let your agent present you with only one insurance company to consider**—he or she should have several different companies and quotes for you to choose from and be able to clearly explain the differences.

Go online. You can get quotes on insurance through online brokers like AccuQuote, InsWeb, Insure.com, QuickQuote, or LLIS.com. You may get less hand-holding through the process than if you were working through a local agent, but you will still have the opportunity to speak with a broker before committing to a plan.

Step 3. Compare Policies

Insurance is something you need to shop for, so look closely at your different quote options. In addition to evaluating cost, you'll need to make sure the insurance company is trustworthy and financially sound. Here's what to look for:

- **Rating.** Look up its rating through S&P (www .standardandpoors.com) or A.M. Best (www.ambest .com). AAA is the highest mark given by S&P; A++ is the highest by A.M. Best.

- **Service.** Look at the level of service they provide. Examine the fine print to see what restrictions apply, how long it would take to file a claim and receive money, and whether there are any negative customer-service reviews online.

And remember, different states have different insurance requirements, so make sure to do your research within your home state.

FEARLESS TIP   *Get a CLUE*

If you are denied coverage as a result of something claimed in the past, the Fair Credit Reporting Act guarantees you a free copy of your CLUE or A-PLUS reports (the reports insurance companies use to see the past seven years of claims). You can get a CLUE report at www.personalreports .lexisnexis.com and an A-PLUS report at www.iso.com.

Health Insurance (Nonnegotiable!)

Why You Should Care

Let's cut to the chase: health insurance is a *must*. And as of 2014 it will be a legal requirement, too. Even if you're between jobs and tempted to wing it for a while, **don't. You cannot let a single day of your life go by uninsured.** Yes, when you're healthy, paying for health insurance might seem like a waste of money. But the reality is that, no matter how healthy you think you are, a health issue could surface without warning at any time—and if you aren't insured, even a minor problem could completely *wipe out* your savings and *destroy* your finances.

A study in the *American Journal of Medicine* found that illness or medical bills contributed to 62 percent of all bankruptcies in 2007.[2] But what's most scary about this statistic is that plenty of these people **weren't going bankrupt because they lacked health insurance.** Most of them had insurance, but *the type they had* **was inadequate to cover their medical costs.** So it's not enough just to be covered; you have to make sure you have the proper coverage that matches your needs.

238 I PROTECT YOURSELF

> ## Uninsured: What It Could Cost You
>
> The stats around the costs of being uninsured are pretty scary. For example, if you go to the hospital with appendicitis, you may well end up with a bill for $30,000—or maybe even as high as $182,000!—while if you have insurance you could pay as little as $1,500.[3] What's more, patients with insurance may well receive better care; a study in the *Annals of Family Medicine* showed that insured patients' hospital stays are significantly longer.[4]

How to Get It

Talk to an

LV

Expert

Given that it's your life on the line here, it's not an exaggeration to say that **health insurance might be *the* most important purchase you ever make**—yet most people don't even know how to shop for it. There's no shame in feeling overwhelmed by this decision: the fine print is notoriously confusing and complicated, and some of the smartest people I know freeze like deer in headlights when confronted with all of the options.

Depending on your situation, you may have several options to consider:

If you have a job. Your employer will probably offer some form of group health insurance, though you may not have a lot of choice in which kind of plan you can get. When you start a new job, you have a certain number of days to sign on to your employer's health insurance plan—it's normally between sixty and ninety days. However, sometimes there is a waiting period before you are fully covered. Some employer-sponsored health coverage also has a specific time period during which you can sign up for a health insurance plan or make changes to your existing plan; this is often called open enrollment, and it typically happens in the fall.

If you're between jobs. You can temporarily extend the health insurance coverage you received from your previous employer. However, this option, a series of federal health benefit provisions called COBRA (Consolidated Omnibus Budget Reconciliation Act), is **expensive.** Another option is to buy an individual or family plan from any private health-care insurer, or even short-term insurance, to cover the gap before you start another job.

If you're a college student. You have several options: your parents can continue to cover you on their plan, you can purchase your university's health plan, or you can buy your own individual plan. You should make this decision based on cost and service offered.

If you're a recent grad. You can stay on your parents' plan until you're twenty-six. Or, if you get a job, you can enroll in any group health insurance sponsored by your employer.

If you have a partner or spouse. You can get your own health insurance or obtain coverage through your partner's plan—make the decision based on cost and coverage.

If you're starting a family soon. You can be covered under your partner or spouse's plan, buy an individual or family plan, or apply for a group health plan from your employer, union, or other organization.

If you're low income. Every state offers public programs to help individuals or families who are struggling financially or cannot get approved for coverage, though the waiting lists can be very long. To find out if you qualify, visit HealthCare.gov.

Note: If you don't fall into any of the above categories, you can buy your own health insurance plan through an organization or a union, though some have restrictions on certain benefits.

Individual plans often have a waiting period (usually between twelve and eighteen months) before they will cover prenatal care and delivery. For some health insurance options, there may be a certain window of time when you can sign up or a waiting period until you're fully covered.

What to Look for in a Health Insurance Plan

There are *so* many crazy, complicated health insurance terms—not to mention acronyms (for example, HMO versus PPO versus POS)—out there, it can make your head spin. My head spins! So let's distill what they mean and what you need to look out for.

Type of plan. Consider how much freedom in choosing providers you'd like, and decide whether an indemnity/fee-for-service plan (which lets you visit any doctor or hospital you want) or a type of managed-care plan (which incentivizes you to visit specific doctors and hospitals) works better for you.

Costs. Consider each plan's premium (the amount you pay to maintain coverage), deductible (what you pay out of pocket before insurance kicks in), co-payments (what you pay up front for a service like an office visit), and coinsurance (the portion you pay for a service before insurance pays the rest). Remember, a high-deductible plan is good if you want a low monthly premium and have savings, and vice versa.

Unnecessary benefits. Avoid expensive benefits, like prenatal care or prescription drugs, if they aren't necessary for you.

Choice of physician. If you have a favorite doctor, figure out which plans he or she accepts and consider buying one. This could be important, for example, if you're planning to start a family and you have an OB/GYN you really trust.

Brand of medication. Some plans cover only generic brands of prescription medicines. Pick the plan that best covers the brand you prefer to take.

FEARLESS LESSON   *The Application Process*

To apply, you'll provide information about yourself—your age, location, and health history—as well as your family members. It can take anywhere from a few days to a few weeks before the insurance company notifies you of its decision.

MONEY MIC: *A Wedding—and a Diagnosis*

I was twenty-nine, happily engaged, and in the midst of wedding planning. And then I got the news.

A nurse at my doctor's office called to follow up on a routine annual physical. "We've reviewed the results from your exam," she told me. "You have papillary carcinoma." She started talking about "next steps," but I barely heard a word.

I hung up the phone and then started Googling "papillary carcinoma." I called back and said, "I'm confused. Are you saying I have thyroid cancer?"

"Yes," she said. It was that moment that it really hit me. She went into further detail about what my diagnosis was and what it meant. It was a very treatable form of cancer but would require surgery and possibly radiation. I broke the news to my fiancé, Tim, and he was as stunned as I was.

There was one saving grace in all of this: I had prepared for this very moment by saving up my emergency fund and having health insurance. I realized a cure would be more than just taking some medication, and I started seeing dollar signs. I hoped I wouldn't have to pay much out of pocket, but even if I did, I would be prepared.

I got to work researching my company's short-term disability plan and reevaluated my flex spending. I looked into what was covered by insurance: 80 percent of most procedures. So I requested estimates on all doctor appointments, biopsies, treatments, and surgery before having them done.

I went into surgery two days before Christmas. When I woke up, the doctors informed me that the cancer had spread to my lymph nodes and that I would need radiation, which would only be partially covered.

During this time I made an important discovery: you can negotiate medical bills. I got a bill for $2,500, but I didn't really understand it. So I called the insurance company, who said there was nothing they could do about it. Then I called the hospital. The insurance department at the hospital said they would investigate. To my surprise, they discovered I had been billed twice for the same surgery and they owed me $250! I also found out that if you prepay your co-pay, they'll give you a break of 10 percent off your bill. For a $750 procedure, that's a big chunk of change.

We recently sat down and added up all the medical costs associated with my thyroid cancer. Without insurance, it would have cost us somewhere from $40,000 to $50,000. With insurance, careful planning, and lots of questions, it cost us just about $4,000. Incidentally, that's about how much we had left over from our wedding budget.

The wedding day went off without a hitch. For me the most significant moment was during our vows, which were the traditional "better or worse . . . richer or poorer." When Tim and I got to the "in sickness and in health" promise, we both got emotional. The magnitude of what we had already been through together really hit us. Since then I've gotten the best news I could imagine: I'm officially cancer free. And financially? We're stronger than ever.

—Becca, 30, Nashville, TN

Renter's Insurance

(Recommended for All Renters!)

Why You Should Care

Renters often feel like insurance isn't something they have to worry about (some don't even know renter's insurance exists!). They figure the landlord will make good if anything bad happens to the property. While landlords are liable for a lot of things, they are not required to pay for your stuff if it gets burglarized or ruined in a fire, flood, or some other disaster. Renters need insurance at least as much as owners! It's just too easy to have something terrible happen that wipes you out.

The good news is that renter's insurance is incredibly affordable. For probably less than the cost of one pizza a month, it will cover you if your annoying neighbor forgets to turn off the tap and floods your closet full of vintage heirlooms or if you accidentally leave your hair straightener on when you leave for work and set your shower curtain on fire. Renter's insurance will not only cover the repairs and replace the stolen or damaged items but also typically put you up in a hotel if your place is temporarily uninhabitable (room service, anyone?).

Most insurance companies offer renter's insurance, so consider starting your search with a company you already hold policies with, where you may receive a discount for buying additional insurance.

What to Look For

We know that the thick packet you receive when you ask for information on any insurance policy is long and complicated, but make sure that you at least read the outline of it, generally the first couple of pages, to figure out what's actually covered. Sometimes acts of God or certain kinds of flood or fire damage aren't covered in the standard policy. You may need riders (i.e., additional coverage) if either of the following applies to you:

☐ You live in an area prone to natural disasters (floods, fires, etc.).

☐ You have jewelry worth over $1,000.

FEARLESS LESSON   *Suggested To-dos After You Get Your Policy*

- Do an inventory of your valuables and how much they are worth. Excel does a nice spreadsheet.

- Take photos of your most valuable items, like furniture and electronics.

- Store your policy somewhere safe along with copies of the photos and inventory. Ideally, put these in a safe deposit box at the bank or at a trusted friend's or relative's house, or scan everything and store it on iCloud.

- Update your policy every year to include any new valuables; otherwise, if you get robbed, those stunning diamond earrings you just got for your birthday will *not* be covered.

Homeowner's Insurance

(Required for Most Homeowners!)

Why You Should Care

Obviously, if you're a homeowner, insurance is critical (and most lenders will require proof of homeowner's insurance when you're financing a mortgage)—and yes, more expensive—simply because you've got more on the line. (Title insurance, too, is almost always required to get a mortgage to buy a house. It insures that you have all of the rights to the property you are buying.) Your lender will let you know what the minimum insurance is, and then you'll need to figure out how much more you want to buy.

Talk to an LV *Expert*

What to Look For

Usually, the basic package will include theft, fire, frozen pipes, electrical shorts, and trees falling through the roof, that kind of thing. What you want beyond that will depend on where your house is. For example, if you live at the foot of a mountain known for avalanches or your block is nicknamed Tornado Alley, you may want some additional riders.

The price of additional protection may give you pause: earthquake insurance can cost between $100 and $3,000 annually depending on where you live, while flood coverage can cost over $500 a year. You should consider whether the annual premiums cost more than potential repairs if disaster should strike. Again, that will all depend on your property and where you live (if you aren't sure what repairs would cost, call a contractor and ask for a quote for your hypothetical damages). So do the math, and if you decide *not* to purchase additional coverage, make sure that you have enough in your emergency fund to cover those repair costs.

FEARLESS TIPS   *Getting the Lowest Premium*

Tip 1   COMPARISON SHOP. To find the best deal, call a variety of companies and get quotes based on your own situation (year built, square footage, price). See if an insurance company you **already use,** like your car insurance company, would be willing to bundle home insurance for a lower rate.

Tip 2   RAISE THE DEDUCTIBLE. If you have some savings in the bank for home emergencies (as you should), you can raise the deductible on your homeowner's insurance to match the amount you have set aside. This is an easy way to lower your premiums, with the security of knowing that you have enough money on hand to cover the deductible if need be.

MONEY MIC: *What a Storm Taught Me About Homeowner's Insurance*

I got home around 4:30 p.m. on the day of the storm, and almost immediately my husband and I looked up at the sky and saw a tree coming straight toward us. It seemed like slow motion—you never think something like this is going to happen to you.

Suddenly, the tree was in middle of the room. Now it was raining in our house—just water pouring in. We went and got every garbage pail we could find and put it under where the rain was falling. And of course we had no power—no one did—so we had to do all of this in the dark.

We tried to just take Hurricane Sandy in stride. In fact, I actually feel lucky, for a few different reasons: no one was hurt, and we were able to sleep in our bedroom that night. But the damage from the storm—physically and financially—was significant.

—Gail, 57, Upper Brookville, NY

In the end, removing the tree from their house alone cost $17,000, plus another $10,000 for the additional eight trees that fell on their property. They also ended up needing a new roof on that part of the house. If they hadn't been insured, they would have had to swallow those costs. All that compared to the few hundred dollars a month they paid for the coverage.

Cost of damage without insurance: **$27,000+**

Cost of damage with insurance: $2,500 deductible + $3,500 annual insurance premiums = $6,000

Disability Insurance (Must Consider!)

Why You Should Care

Want to take your self-protection to the next level? This insurance will replace your income if you become disabled and can't work. Think it just won't happen to you? It's terrifying, but just over one in four of today's twenty-year-olds will become disabled before age sixty-seven.[5] I don't know about you, but I do *not* like those odds.

Disability insurance is **especially** important for people with high-risk jobs or hobbies (if you're an avid mountain climber, for example) and those in a single-income household (to replace the sole earner's income if something happens to him or her).

What to Look For

When you're looking for disability insurance, there are both short- and long-term policies available. The point of disability insurance is to cover you when you can't work, so first and foremost you need to look at what the policy defines as work. There are two big categories: "own-occupation" coverage, which states that you will receive insurance money if you are too disabled to perform *your* job. The alternative is "any-occupation," which kicks in only when you're unable to perform *any* job.

Why You Need Own-Occupation Coverage

If this seems like silly semantics, think again. Imagine, for example, a business executive salaried at $300,000 who sustains a brain injury but is told that she won't receive disability insurance because, even though she can't work at her old job, she could still work in the fast-food industry at $10 an hour. In this case she would be properly protected only with "own-occupation" coverage.

FEARLESS LESSON   *Application Process*

The most affordable way to get disability insurance is usually through your company, so consult your HR department and see what it offers.

 MONEY MIC: *My Lifeline*

In 2004 I was in my early forties, living alone in New Jersey and working as a home mortgage consultant. My insurance agency advised me to look at my options for potential policies, including disability insurance.

I already had disability insurance through my job, but it would never have covered my income were I to become disabled, so I took my agent's advice and purchased a long-term policy to supplement the one I already had. Together the two policies cost me about $300 a month.

Fast-forward two years to 2006, when I was diagnosed as bipolar. I tried to go back to my job but couldn't make it work, and my doctor put me on permanent disability. I hadn't even realized that the insufficient policy through my job was a short-term policy and only covered me for two years. After that, my long-term policy will kick in and cover me until I'm sixty-five.

My disability insurance pays me about $4,100 a month, and I'm so grateful. The bottom line is that without this policy, I couldn't afford to live. —Ruby, 48, Manalapan, NJ

Auto Insurance

(Have a Car? 100 Percent Must)

Why You Should Care

If you own a car, obviously you are required by law to have auto insurance. But this isn't just some silly rule. This coverage is critical—it protects you financially from any damage done to *and* by your car.

What to Look For

If you have a car, you should already have car insurance in place. But do you have the best rates? Here's how to find out: if you answer "yes" to any of the below questions, it's time to chat with your insurance agent ASAP.[6]

- **Does your policy cover a teenager with a GPA of 3.0 or higher?** On some plans you can save up to 25 percent.

- **Are you a teacher?** You may be eligible to save up to 7.5 percent.

- **Have you taken a defensive driving course?** You may save up to 10 percent.

- **Do you have more than one policy with the agent or insurer?** You may save up to 25 percent.

- **Does your car have safety features (like air bags, antilock brakes, and an alarm)?** Save up to 10 percent.

- **Are you willing to keep a black box on your car (or your teen's car) that tracks driving habits?** Save 10 percent to 15 percent.

- **Are you a safe driver?** Some insurance providers offer discounts of up to 10 percent for an accident-free record.

If none of those situations apply to you, don't worry! There are still a few other ways to cut down on your auto insurance bill:

Raise your deductible. It seems counterintuitive to offer to pay *more* money should something go wrong, but raising the amount you're on the hook for to $500 will save you 15 percent to 30 percent. Raising it to $1,000 will save you 40 percent or more. Why the savings? By raising your deductible, you lower the potential for the insurance company to pay up. If you do this, make sure you've set aside the funds to actually cover the deductible should anything happen.

Drop collision and comprehensive coverage. Do this only if your car is worth less than $1,000 or what you would pay in premiums in a year. If you have an expensive car, please don't drop your collision insurance just because you think you're a great driver; there are lots of crazies on the road, so don't assume you are immune to accidents!

Get a car with a low "loss history." A car's "loss history" is a measure of how well the drivers of cars of that make and model typically drive. Use Insure.com's car insurance comparison tool to find yours. If it's low, you might be eligible for a lower insurance rate.

MONEY MIC: *How My Detective Work Paid Off*

In 2010, our entire neighborhood was flooded. My car, which was parked outside, ended up with more than 1 foot of water inside, resulting in a total loss. While the insurance company paid book value, I did a little digging on my own and discovered there were two book values. The insurance company promised me the lower one. I brought it to their attention and eventually received the higher book value. While I greatly appreciated the check, a little extra digging netted me more than $2,000 extra.

—Frank, 56, Wilton Manors, FL

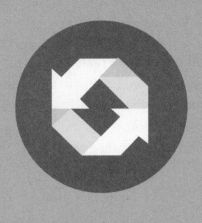

Life Insurance

(The Ultimate Way to Protect Your Family)

Why You Should Care

There are so many ways to be a good spouse and parent: washing the dishes unasked, supporting your loved one's ambitions and dreams . . . and getting life insurance. Compared to health insurance, which you use every time you pick up a prescription, you rarely have a reason to think about life insurance. But that doesn't make it any less important. Life insurance is especially critical today, as more families have been forced into living on a single income due to the recession. In a 2010 survey, 40 percent of households with children under eighteen said they would have trouble meeting financial obligations if a primary breadwinner passed away. Unfortunately, this research also showed that individual life insurance ownership was at a fifty-year low.[7] So buck the trend and get some!

Life insurance works just like other types of insurance—car, home, and health—in that you pay a monthly premium in case something bad or unexpected happens, in this case the death of an income earner and/or spouse. But life insurance is a little different too, in that it packs a heavy emotional punch. On one hand, taking steps to prepare for one's own death can be psychologically very uncomfortable. (I know I don't love the topic!) On the other hand, having life insurance means that you're sparing your children the added burden of financial uncertainty while they are also dealing with a major emotional loss. Think about it this way: your life insurance policy isn't for you; it's for other people in your life who depend on you and whom you love.

Clearly, money can't "replace" a deceased loved one the way it can a car or a stolen computer. But it *can* replace—at least partially—the income that loved one was contributing to the household, the income his or her surviving spouse and children depend on to stay financially secure. For me, the peace of mind that comes from knowing your family will be taken care of is priceless.

Consider Life Insurance If . . .

You are working, but your spouse isn't. If your spouse isn't working, it will take some time for him or her to get back into the workforce if you die and he or she suddenly needs income to live on. Life insurance can replace the income of the earner and at the least ease the widow's or widower's transition back into working life. The reverse is of course true if you're the one not working and depend on your spouse's income.

You have young children (especially if you or your spouse is a stay-at-home parent). If one spouse is taking care of the children and the earner passes away, the widower or widow will now need to not only transition back into working life but also pay for child care, an enormous expense. In this situation, policies should actually be taken out for both parents, even the one not currently working. That's because if the nonworking spouse dies, the earner will also need additional money for child care and other newly necessary expenses, like housecleaning or ordering takeout.

Even if you're both working, there are immediate and long-term extra expenses that come with the death of a spouse. There's a barrage of things to cover: the funeral, mortgage payments, school or college tuition, and car payments and remaining credit-card debt that were feasible only on a dual income. Life insurance is a way of ensuring that creditors don't come knocking should you suffer the premature death of a spouse.

You are single and supporting family members. If you are supporting a parent or other family member, life insurance would replace your support in the event of your death.

You are single with cosigned or large debts (like private student loans). If you have any loans that wouldn't be written off if you were to pass away, such as cosigned federal student loans, most private student loans, auto loans, or a mortgage, life insurance can take care of the debt so that whichever family member or friend cosigned the loan isn't stuck holding the bag. (Federal student loans with no cosigner are generally written off upon the borrower's death.)

You have a mortgage. A life insurance policy can help ensure that your estate will be able to prevent your property from going into foreclosure.

You co-own a business but don't have sufficient assets to buy out the other partner(s). If you have signed an agreement under which you would take over a business upon a partner's death but don't have the assets to do so, you should take out life insurance on your business partner to make sure that the business stays open while you get the cash together.

FEARLESS LESSON　*When Not to Get Life Insurance*

In my opinion, the only people who *don't* need life insurance are singles who have no one depending on them for income and no major outstanding liabilities.

What to Look For

There are a few different types of life insurance policies, including "term" (meaning good for a certain number of years) and "whole" (good for the entire life of the insured). The latter is of course the more costly option, so for most people looking to use insurance to take the place of a lost income during their working years, **term insurance is the way to go.**

When you go term, you'll need to select the length of time for which you want the policy premiums to stay the same; usually this ranges from fifteen to thirty years. I recommend you cover yourself through age sixty-five or through your children's time in college (whichever is longer).

You'll also need to determine how much coverage you need. This is entirely up to you and depends on how much you think your survivors will need to maintain a comfortable lifestyle. But here's my good rule of thumb: **buy a policy with a cash payout of seven to ten times your current yearly income.** For a more precise figure, you can add up the value of all the financial obligations your family would need to meet if you passed away (funeral, extra child care, lost income, etc.), then subtract the amount you currently have in savings, retirement funds, investments, and other life insurance policies you already have on your life that would pass to your family or spouse.

If your employer offers a plan, make sure to check the size of the benefit. A payout of $30,000 may seem like a lot, but it likely won't be enough to sustain your family for long.

FEARLESS TIP *Employee Perks*

Many employer plans will insure you with no medical exam—a huge win. However, if you want to take the policy with you after you leave that job, you might have to pass a medical exam.

FEARLESS LESSON *How Do Life Insurance Benefits Work?*

In the event of your death, your beneficiary (the person you designated to receive the benefit) makes a claim, and the insurance company writes him or her a check for the amount of the policy (called a "benefit"), either in a lump sum or in regular payments. Oh, and another bonus: this benefit is almost never subject to federal or state income taxes, which will make the money last longer during a difficult time.

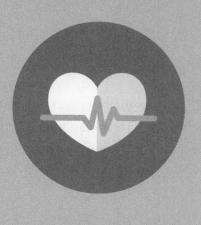

Long-Term-Care Insurance

Why You Should Care

Long-term-care insurance will cover the costs if you or a loved one becomes incapacitated and needs perpetual care, such as entering a nursing home. Given the uncertainty of the Social Security system, this is worth considering if you can afford it and are still young enough that costs won't be astronomical.

The younger you buy it, the better, because if you lock in a rate early, it can actually be affordable. The cost doesn't seem so intimidating once you compare it to the cost of a nursing home. A 2011 MassMutual study found that the national average annual cost of a private room in a nursing home is over $87,000![8] And you thought college was expensive . . .

What to Look For

In general, when comparing different policies, look out for what levels of care are covered by the policy, where you can receive care, how long benefits are paid for, and what amounts are covered. Keep an eagle eye out for any policy exclusions (like common illnesses or requirements to spend a certain amount of time in the hospital before you can access benefits). In addition, make sure to check if the policy includes the cost of medication and medical supplies on top of paying for caregivers.

Umbrella Insurance

(If You Have Significant Assets or High Net Worth)

Why You Should Care

An umbrella policy is one that covers you when your liability is higher than the total coverage from your other policies. So if your homeowner's insurance covers up to $300,000 and you are sued for $500,000, for example, you'd use the $300,000 liability coverage of homeowner's first, and then umbrella would pick up the balance.

This insurance often makes the most sense for people with a high net worth. Essentially, it sits on top of an auto or homeowner's policy and helps protect you (and your assets) from any rulings against you in a liability lawsuit. Did you know that such rulings can even garnish your future wages, so that they'll be applied directly to pay damages? If it's hard to imagine getting sued, think of all the driving you do and all of the people who come through your home (perhaps babysitters, gardeners, neighbors)—

if you accidentally hit someone, or if something goes wrong and someone gets injured while on your property, **it could be on you.**

The more money you have, **the more of a target you are,** so I recommend considering an umbrella policy once you have substantial assets. It's also something to consider if you're in a position that involves taking on liability (like if you sit on a board of directors).

What to Look For

Policies are sold in increments of $1 million and cap out at $3 million.

Make sure that your underlying liability insurance meets the requirements of your umbrella policy. For example, your umbrella policy may not kick in until the five hundred thousandth dollar you owe. If your underlying policy covers only $300,000 in liability, you'd be responsible for that $200,000 in the doughnut hole. Make sure you have an expert help you if you have any questions.

Talk to an LV *Expert*

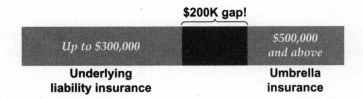

$200K gap!

Up to $300,000 — $500,000 and above

Underlying liability insurance — **Umbrella insurance**

Whew, okay, that section on insurance wasn't so bad, was it? Now that you know what types of insurance you need and what to look for, it's time to get your . . .

Docs in a Row

You thought insurance was the least fun topic we could discuss . . . but now we break out the list of documents you need! Woo-hoo!

Sorry, we have to. You can't call yourself fully protected if you don't have your critical paperwork done. Below are the six things you need to have under control.

1. **Beneficiary forms.** A beneficiary form lets you indicate who you would like money to be transferred to upon your death—even if you don't have a will. If you have any of the following account types, you've likely filled this out already: a 401(k) or retirement accounts through work, life insurance policies, IRAs,

annuity accounts, and 529 college savings accounts. If you're married, it's common to list your spouse as your beneficiary (and if you want to do otherwise, you may be required to have your spouse sign off on that). This saves you money because it keeps your assets out of probate court.

What to do: Ask for a copy of your beneficiary form for each account and make sure it's properly filled out. Save your own copy.

2 **TOD/POD instruction.** TOD (transfer on death) and POD (payable on death) are other ways you can transfer assets to a beneficiary without a will. TODs are typically used for any brokerage accounts that do not have a beneficiary form in place, and PODs are for bank accounts (like your checking and savings). Having these forms allows you to avoid probate even if your financial situation does not yet require a full-blown will or trust.

What to do: Make sure all accounts that do not have a beneficiary form have a TOD or POD instruction in place.

3 **Living will.** A living will lets you communicate your medical preferences to your loved ones. This is awful to think about, but it helps simplify any tough decisions your family and friends may have to make if something happens to you. A living will includes naming your health-care proxy—the person responsible for carrying out your living will. We recommend choosing a loved one or even an unbiased adviser who can remain neutral.

What to do: Staying in control of your health-care decisions is a powerful tool, so make sure you have an up-to-date living will.

4 **Power of attorney.** This document gives someone else the right to make decisions for you (if you're no longer able to). It can cover both legal affairs and health-care decisions.

　What to do: A power of attorney is recommended once you're married, but even if you're single, it's something to consider if you may be in a situation where someone will have to act on your behalf.

5 **Last will and testament.** A will guides the court in making decisions for you after your death and helps ensure that your wishes come to fruition. It's a critical tool for parents, as it assigns legal guardianship of your minor children.

　What to do: If you own a home or have children, you will need a proper will. If you're not yet in that position, your beneficiary forms will work for now!

6 **Trust documents.** A trust is like a will, in that it outlines what you want to happen to your assets upon your death. Unlike a will, assets in a trust do not go through probate (which means the court cannot interfere with your decisions). It allows you total control over the passing of your assets to heirs.

Talk to an LV Expert

　What to do: Trusts are recommended when you have children and/or a complex financial situation (e.g., children from multiple marriages).

> **FEARLESS** TIP   *Consider Getting a Safe-Deposit Box*
>
> As the name implies, this is a safe place to store sensitive documents, such as your birth certificate, paper stock or bond certificates, and copies of insurance policies. If you have documents like these lying around, consider protecting them at your most trusted brick-and-mortar bank. It only costs around $25 per year, less than a penny a day![9]

Wrapping Up

Now you know what insurance you may need to buy, what policies you need to update, and what docs you need securely stored in your safe-deposit box. You should feel fantastic about checking off these to-dos. Nothing feels as good as knowing you and your family are protected from life in all its chaos.

Too often, insurance and estate planning are one of those "Oh, I should probably get around to doing that" things that linger in the back of your mind, quietly nagging you for years—decades, even. And we finally just got through them! It's the best thing you could have done with your time. Let's check off those boxes on your "financial plan" checklist. Connect with one of our Learn-Vest Program experts if you need help following through.

Talk to an

LV

Expert

What You've Accomplished

✓   Determined what insurance you need to buy

✓   Read up on how to get the insurance and what to look for

✓   Organized and securely stored important insurance-related documents

Questions for Your Expert

If you still have questions about anything we've covered in this section, write them here and then go to www.learnvest.com/financiallyfearless for answers.

I still don't understand . . .

_____

_____

Where do I find . . .

_____

_____

What should I do about my . . .

_____

_____

Talk to an

LV

Expert

Examples:

In addition to health insurance, I need three other insurance policies I don't currently have, but I definitely do not have enough money to purchase all of them right now. How do I prioritize?

My spouse just started a new job—how do we evaluate which health-care plan is best for our family?

My insurance broker recommended "whole" life insurance over "term." Which is right for me?

PROTECT YOURSELF

from

OTHERS

You know that saying about hoping for the best but preparing for the worst? That's what you want to do when it comes to money and other people. I can't even count the number of stories I've heard about relationships—both personal and professional—that were ruined by money. These stories are intense, dramatic, and often heartbreaking. So let's start with some story time.

MONEY MIC: *Engagement Gone Wrong*

A few years ago, I got engaged to a man whose family was from Greece. His parents agreed to pay for the wedding if we had it there. My fiancé and I purchased some of the things we needed for the big day in cash. I put the dress, the plane tickets, the honeymoon expenses, and some other incidentals on my credit card, banking on repayment from my in-laws-to-be. I flew to Europe two weeks before the wedding to prepare. There were many misunderstandings, mostly due to the language barrier, but also in some core values. As a result, we ... drumroll, please ... called off the wedding.

When I left to get married I'd also quit my job, with assurance from my employer that the position would (probably) be available when I returned. Oh, and we moved all of our things from our apartment into storage so we could save money on rent during our extended honeymoon. Yes, I literally had no contingency plan.

When it ended, I had to hitch a plane solo back to the States *from Europe in the dead of summer, back to no job, no home, and with $15,000 in credit-card debt. I was jobless for three months and had to move back in with my parents. I took the first job I was offered, at a nonprofit that barely paid me enough to get by. Adding insult to injury, my Prince Charming went on our honeymoon in Europe by himself!*

Four years later, I am still paying this debt off at a rate of hundreds of dollars per month thanks to all the interest. (No, neither he nor his family would help me—good thing we broke up, right?) This debt represents a part of my life that I would like to be finished with. I would rather be using the money to go to graduate school. How can I get out of this hole?

—Jessica, 32, Santa Barbara, CA

The moral: you can't always prevent fights, firings, breakups, and sour business dealings from happening. But you can prevent them from completely wrecking you and your wallet. You know this already, but I am going to repeat it because it's *that* important: **you *must* be able to support yourself financially.** I'll walk you through the steps you need to take to stay in control of your money—no matter who you're dealing with.

Protect Yourself from . . . Your Employer

There's a reason for unions, OSHA, and the many protections out there for whistle-blowers and those who have been abused in one way or another by their employers. Unfortunately, there are a lot of different ways your employer can screw you (to learn more about your rights, visit the Department of Labor's website, www.dol.gov), but the main issue we'll talk about in this section is your employment contract.

There are only two ways to seriously change your financial picture: you can earn more, or you can spend less. I've already focused on helping you spend smarter and spend less. So now let's take a little time to figure out how you can earn more money. Negotiating your worth is a critical life skill (applicable in *so* many ways!), so it's really important that you hone this and become a pro over time.

The fact is, your salary *has* to go up over time. Not only are your work responsibilities hopefully increasing (to merit a salary increase), but you at least need to keep pace with inflation (about 3 percent a year)[1] to maintain the power of your dollars. One of your best opportunities to get a significant raise in salary, however, is when you take a new job. These situations don't come along every day, so it's critical not to blow it. Here I'll show you what you need to make sure your new employer doesn't take advantage of you and get the best employment terms possible.

What Goes into an Employment Contract (and What You Can Negotiate)

When you take the new job, **you may not think of your employment offer letter as a financial contract, but it is,** as its terms essentially dictate your earning power. There's a lot that goes into that original contract—and therefore a lot that can be negotiated along the way as you move up the ladder. Here are the key elements to consider:

1. **Salary.** Let's start with the obvious. When you sign on to a new job, you should be sure to ask about whether you might be eligible for incentives, bonuses, raise schedules, or anything else that might bump up your take-home pay. If you're already on the job, this is an obvious point to bring up at a review. Have you been killing it at work? Your paycheck and bonuses should reflect that.

2. **Flexibility.** Is your commute really draining you? Or are you a parent who wants to spend more time at home with your kids? See if your company is willing to let you telecommute or work more flexible hours.

3. **Vacation and sick days.** Do you get three weeks of vacation right off the bat or none until you've logged five years? Can you roll over vacation days from year to year? If you go over your allotted vacation, can you take extra days unpaid? All this is good to know before you ink an employment deal. And if your

employer can't bump up your salary, perhaps the company can give you extra time off to compensate.

4 **Education.** Some companies have tuition-reimbursement programs that will let you take evening classes to get an additional degree or new skills or certifications. Find out what your company will pay for, and if it doesn't currently reimburse for a course or degree you think might enhance your value to the company, don't hesitate to ask for a special exception to the policy. Never hurts to ask! And again, be sure to get the decision in writing (if it goes your way, of course).

5 **Title.** You may not care *now* whether your official title is "associate" or "assistant manager" (or for you *The Office* lovers out there, "assistant regional manager" versus "assistant *to* the regional manager"), but it may matter a great deal when you're looking for work again down the road. Make sure your title reflects your level of experience and the level of work you're doing on an ongoing basis.

6 **Benefits.** These may include health, dental, or life insurance; retirement-plan savings matching; or stock options in the company. If the benefits package is good, it can add *huge value* to a salary.

How to Negotiate Your Salary

Whether you're starting a new job or it's review time, here are some tips for coming out ahead:

Tip 1   **Know what you're worth.** Figure out the average range for your position. Check websites like Salary.com, look at ads your company places for other jobs, and discreetly ask a mentor what range you should be expecting. Plan to ask for a number a bit higher than what you really want so you can meet in the middle, and use a very specific number that suggests you've put research into it. For example, if you're currently at $50,000 and want to be making about $55,000, ask for $57,500.

Tip 2   **Time it right.** Set up a time in advance rather than grabbing your boss on his or her way to a meeting and stammering, "By the way . . ." And be sure to put the meeting on your calendars.

Tip 3   **Prove your value.** Start by telling your boss how much you enjoy working for the company, and be prepared to explain why you deserve a raise. Talk about your recent accomplishments and how the company is benefiting from them. (Whether or not you're currently looking for a raise, always keep a private journal of your accomplishments to refer to when needed.) Ask yourself these questions to quantify your contribution to the company:

- Have you saved your company time or money? If so, how much?

- Have you added to company profits through a client you brought on or an initiative you proposed? How much did you make the company? How much business did you bring in?

- Have you exceeded the metrics your boss set when she hired you (e.g., you were hired to increase Web traffic by 100 percent but your projects increased traffic by 250 percent)?

- What kinds of projects have you taken on beyond the scope of your job?

- Are you the person who covers for your boss or others regularly?

Be sure to bring any documentation of these numbers, whether in chart, graph, or spreadsheet form.

Tip 4   **Have a plan B.** Be confident and ready, but also consider your strategy if your request is denied, which sometimes happens for a million reasons beyond your control. Remember to remain gracious and dignified, no matter what happens. If your boss says that a raise isn't right at the moment, think about whether there is anything else you can ask for, such as flexible work hours, profit sharing, paid time off, or tuition reimbursement. Remember that "no" is usually "no for now." Consider asking, "Is there anything more I can do to add value to this company?" or "What would I need to do for your answer to be different in six months?" Agree on a time to revisit the topic with your superiors, whether it's three or six months in the future. It goes without saying that in the meantime you'll want to work as hard as you can so you don't give anyone a reason to say no. **And never forget that enthusiasm and a great attitude are** *critical.* If you get turned down, resist the urge to sulk.

Protect Yourself from . . .

Your Significant Other

I know what you're thinking. Talking about money is *so* unromantic (take it from me—a *huge* romantic at heart!). Remember when candlelit dinners on Friday were not followed by Saturday-morning conversations about credit-card bills and insurance deductibles? Well, these conversations may not be sexy, but they *are* crucial to long-term happiness. They're the only way to ensure that you're protected financially if something goes awry. Better yet, they can protect your relationship from falling apart at the first sign of money trouble.

When you really think about it, sharing your finances is just about as intimate as it gets. Whether you're just engaged or have been married for years, your future is going to include lots of big, joint financial decisions. Talking through costs and plans now will be great practice for the rest of your life.

Your Shared Values

To start, let's see if you and your partner are on the same page when it comes to money. Financial psychologists have a variety of strategies for getting couples to sort out their priorities together. One popular and helpful method uses decks of cards with values printed on each card.[2]

At LearnVest we've created our own take on these cards with the six money values we see couples discuss over and over again. They are stability, luxury, ambition, freedom, generosity, and legacy. Here's what they mean:

Stability. You value having extra money in the bank, the right insurance, and a solid plan that gives you a real cushion. You put sleeping well at night above everything.

Luxury. You value the best in life, the nicest things, the prettiest homes.

Ambition. You value being able to take risks and see how your money can work for you. Through starting your own venture or investing in unique ideas, you want the opportunity to take your finances to the next level.

Freedom. You value being in control of your money. You care about autonomy and being able to let your money do what *you* would like—whether it's being able to quit your job, travel at any time, or make your own lifestyle.

Generosity. You value giving back to your community, your family, your favorite causes. You want to be able to be charitable to those around you.

Legacy. You value giving your children everything—the best education, endless opportunities—and you want to leave them and your grandchildren with as much as possible.

Your Values

Stability	Freedom
Luxury	Generosity
Ambition	Legacy

Your Partner's Values

Stability	Freedom
Luxury	Generosity
Ambition	Legacy

Your Values

You value being in control of your money. You care about autonomy and being able to let your money do what *you* would like—whether it's being able to quit your job, travel at any time, or make your own lifestyle.

You value having extra money in the bank, the right insurance, and a solid plan that gives you a real cushion. You put sleeping well at night above everything.

You value giving back to your community, your family, your favorite causes. You want to be able to be charitable to those around you.

You value the best in life, the nicest things, the prettiest homes.

You value giving your children everything—the best education, endless opportunities—and you want to leave them and your grandchildren with as much as possible.

You value being able to take risks and see how your money can work for you. Through starting your own venture or investing in unique ideas, you want the opportunity to take your finances to the next level.

Your Partner's Values

You value being in control of your money. You care about autonomy and being able to let your money do what *you* would like—whether it's being able to quit your job, travel at any time, or make your own lifestyle.

You value having extra money in the bank, the right insurance, and a solid plan that gives you a real cushion. You put sleeping well at night above everything.

You value giving back to your community, your family, your favorite causes. You want to be able to be charitable to those around you.

You value the best in life, the nicest things, the prettiest homes.

You value giving your children everything—the best education, endless opportunities—and you want to leave them and your grandchildren with as much as possible.

You value being able to take risks and see how your money can work for you. Through starting your own venture or investing in unique ideas, you want the opportunity to take your finances to the next level.

Here's how this activity works: Cut out the cards. Each person ranks their set of cards in order of importance to them, and then the couples see where they agree and where they don't. For example, maybe you both have security as your number one priority. But maybe one of you has security and the other has freedom. That may be a source of conflict.

This exercise is not just an excuse to start talking about money with your significant other; **it's an opportunity to more deeply understand each other's core financial values.** If your values are not aligned you will be pulling each other in different directions *every day* of your relationship with dozens of micro-decisions. As a result, you won't be a financially strong or unified couple—a fact that will only be compounded by the addition of mortgages, children, and whatever other financial obligations come your way.

Of course, few couples are going to rank these priorities in the *exact* same order. (If you do, well, hallelujah! My husband and I could learn a thing or two from you!) What *does* matter is that you understand *why* your significant other prioritizes something, so you can understand it and show that you care. You need to talk through *why* you chose what you chose and analyze where your priorities are at odds. Knowing this will help you have the right conversations about where you want to spend moving forward.

Financial Infidelity

Did you know that money is the *number one* (I repeat: number one!) thing couples fight about?[3] Yeah, you're not the only ones who fight about money. It's all of us. Even more dangerous to a relationship than openly fighting about money, however, is financial infidelity, when one of you hides bank accounts or spending or debt from the other. Look, I get why people try to keep those secrets: no one likes to own up to mistakes they've made about money; plus, it's been found that when one partner feels like the other spends money foolishly, the couple is 45 percent more likely to divorce.[4] Even so, secrecy and deception, especially when perpetuated for long periods of time, can be infinitely more harmful to the marriage in the long run.

Okay, so that's a bunch of bad news, but the good news is that talking to your partner about money is good not only for your bank account but also for your sex life and your chance of staying together. That's because when you're talking about money, it's not just money you're talking about: it's trust, love, and security. That's what makes it especially tough sometimes—and so very important.

I recommend sitting down on a regular basis (at least once a year) and dealing with your money. Keep the tone light, and have the conversation when you're both relaxed and not on edge after a hard day. Flattery will get you everywhere, so it won't hurt to compliment your partner about anything you can think of, whether it's his or her frugality or his or her great savings plan. Figure out what your shared goals are and whether you're both doing what you need to in order to get there. Approach dealing with money as just another one of those things you do together, like walking the dog or watching TV. The more open and honest you are about money, the happier you'll both be.

Here are some prompts to get the conversation started.

Ten "Money Talk" Questions to Ask

1. Do you feel like we're in good shape right now, moneywise? Are we on a good path?

2. What's the next major purchase you see us making together?

3. Do you have any worries about money, anything that keeps you up at night?

4. Is there any spending we should cut back on?

5 What's your vision for our retirement?

6 Where do we see our careers going in the next few years?

7 How long do we want to stay in our current living situation?

8 What financial goals are our top priorities right now?

9 Is our current money system working?

10 Is there anything we can be doing to make our lives better?

FEARLESS LESSON *How to Manage a Joint Bank Account*

When two people combine their money, sometimes they completely merge their accounts into one. Other times they keep totally separate accounts. But there's also a hybrid model that allows you to contribute equally regardless of differing incomes. (If you ever do split up, it's a lot easier to unmerge your finances.)

Here's how it works: Each of you puts 75 percent of your income into a joint account that you use for bills you share, like rent, electricity, and vacations together. You each put 25 percent into your own accounts, which you use for your own expenses, like clothes and drinks out at bars. (If one of you is not currently working or bringing in income, establish a fair guideline for joint and individual spending that's in line with your available resources.)

That way, you avoid fights over whether you should have bought that new iPad. You decide how you spend your 25 percent. You both decide how you spend your joint money. This works well for a lot of couples since you get to have the feeling of both being independent and being part of a team. And it's way easier to surprise each other with gifts!

Visit LearnVest.com/financiallyfearless for my video explaining the process!

Three Ways to Manage Your Money

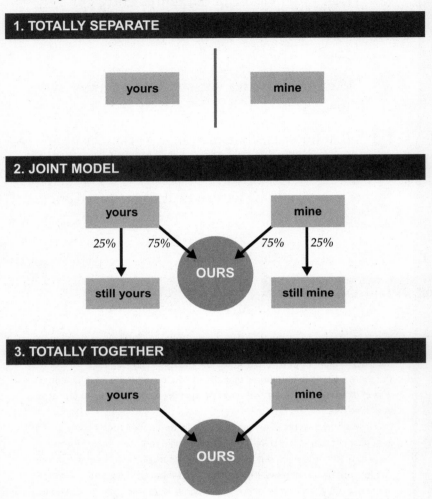

Getting Hitched

Wedding documents don't include just save-the-date and thank-you cards. The following chart outlines some paperwork you should take care of come engagement time. These items may not be as colorful, but they are crucial to protecting yourself financially at this critical juncture in your life.

What you can do now

Get your credit scores	You should know each other's credit scores, especially if one partner has significantly better credit than the other. Having a good credit score can save you thousands of dollars.
Get homeowner's or renter's insurance	If you're already cohabiting, get homeowner's or renter's insurance. Because insurers often give discounts for putting more than one product (e.g., two cars and a house) on their policies, consider having your homeowner's insurance through the same company that does your auto insurance. (However, you may have to be married to get your auto insurance together, so you may want to wait till after the wedding.)

What you can research now and complete after the wedding

Get the greatest health insurance coverage for the lowest cost	If you are both on employer-sponsored health insurance, find out now what the coverage is for married couples on each plan. Then compare and select the best plan for the price. If one of you has insurance and the other doesn't, add the uninsured person.
Put your cars on the same auto insurance	Data show that married people are less likely to have car accidents, so insurance companies often give discounts for having two cars on the same policy.
Get life insurance	Because getting married normally creates some financial dependency between spouses, you should get life insurance for any spouse earning an income. That will protect the other person in the event that one of you dies prematurely. We know it's not cheerful, but it's a must-do to protect yourself.
Draw up or amend your will	If you already have a will, redo it as soon as you get married, including your spouse. If you don't have a will, you should draw one up together. Use a site like LegalZoom to do it inexpensively.
Draw up your living will, health-care proxy, and HIPAA authorization form	If you don't already have a living will and health-care proxy, draw them up now. Also, give your fiancé(e) HIPAA authorization, so he or she can access your protected medical information.
Change your withholding	At work, right after you're married, change your withholding on your W-4 form to add your spouse as an exemption. This will ensure the proper amount in taxes is withdrawn from your paycheck.
Use your new filing status	The next time you file your taxes, change your filing status to "married" and decide with your spouse whether you should file jointly (the more common scenario) or separately.
Name your spouse as a beneficiary	In all of your financial accounts, name your spouse as a beneficiary, which is the person or entity named as the inheritor of your property or assets in the event of your death.
Set up a joint account	If you go with a joint account, you can set one up once you're married.

To Prenup or Not to Prenup . . .

Let me start by saying that I'm a big believer in marriage, and I'm an absolute romantic. That said, prenups are something every couple should at least *consider*. This is an incredibly personal and private decision, but it's one you need to make. If you decide not to have one, fine, but I don't want you to not have one because you felt like it was too icky a topic to bring up. Talk it out, weigh the pros and cons, and make the best decision for you and your spouse, together.

What Is a Prenup?

A prenuptial agreement is a legally binding agreement that a couple signs before getting married, stating how assets will be divided in the event of divorce or death. A prenup might seem like the opposite of romantic, but it's becoming part of standard wedding planning. I recognize it's not only a financial decision but also an emotional and deeply personal one, but look at it this way: if you don't feel comfortable talking to the person you're about to spend your life with about this, what other important issues are you sweeping under the rug? Prenups can cover anything regarding your finances or possessions, including:

- How to split finances

- Who gets to keep certain items

- How to divide a home fairly

- How debt gets divvied up

- Financial support for a spouse who gives up a career to raise kids

- How long a spouse and/or kids can stay in the house after a divorce

- Support payments, including settlement or alimony

- Inheritance for kids from a previous marriage

When a Prenup Might Make Sense

1 **You make considerably more than your spouse.** This is a pretty obvious one—though if your spouse makes considerably more than you, you may *not* want to consider pushing for one.

2 **Your partner has a lot of debt and you don't.** If you don't clearly define whose debt is whose before the wedding, you may be stuck with it after a divorce.

3 **You have kids from a previous marriage.** A prenup will allow you to clearly allocate your assets for their benefit. **This is a very important time to consider this.**

4 **You envision leaving the workforce someday to care for your children.** And in doing so, limit your income and earning power for a period of your marriage. A prenup can lay claim to some of your partner's income accrued during this time.

If you decide to pursue a prenup, check out affordable resources at LegalZoom.com.

If you decide that a prenup isn't right for you, you're not quite done yet. You still need some plan to protect your finances if your relationship ends. If your significant other walked out tomorrow, what would happen? Are your savings accounts in your name, too? Who has access to the bank accounts? By **no means** do I want to encourage major relationship paranoia; just be aware and smart about the joint money decisions you make before you walk down the aisle.

Little-known fact: if you decide against a prenup before your wedding, you can always reevaluate after. If your financial situation changes down the road or you just have a change of heart about the idea of getting your if-we-break-up money agreement in writing, postnups *are* an option. In fact, they're increasingly popular. According to the American Academy of Matrimonial Lawyers, 51 percent of divorce attorneys say that postnups have been on the rise in recent years.[5] A postnup offers essentially the same protection as a prenup. The only difference is that it happens after a wedding.

FEARLESS TIP   *Are You Changing Your Name?*

If so, get a new Social Security card from the Social Security Administration. It's important to notify the SSA of your name change so your retirement account is properly credited with your earnings. Get a new driver's license and passport, too, so there are no hang-ups when you plan to travel.

FEARLESS TIPS   *Moving in Together?*

Tip 1   It's unsexy, I know, but consider forming a cohabitation agreement to formalize your financial responsibilities and commitments. Go here for an easy starter document: www.legalzoom.com/legalforms/Cohabitation-Agreement.html.

Tip 2   If you're living together but not married, be careful about opening lines of credit together. Unlike in a marriage, where there are some clear-cut laws, one of you could be saddled with significant debt if the relationship ends.

Protect Yourself from . . .

Your Friends and Family

We love all our friends and family, but let's face it: some are better for our bank accounts than others. Money-toxic friends are those who tend to put you in situations that encourage you to overspend or that strip you of control over your money. This can include ordering lots of expensive drinks on a communal tab, suggesting highly pricey group activities that leave you feeling peer-pressured to do things you can't afford, or even giving you a present that's uncomfortably costly—making you feel obligated to reciprocate with something equally expensive (I suspect you know who these people are). According to one study, 21 percent of people have felt pressured to keep up with friends in their spending, and 20 percent said they have had a "friend breakup" over a money dispute.[6]

At some point, everyone encounters a sticky money situation. You borrow or lend money without a clear plan for payback. A cousin invites you to her destination wedding—and you just can't say no. Your coworker puts you on the spot and asks you to buy tickets to a pricey gala supporting his charity for underprivileged kids. There's no point in blaming them for putting you in this situation. Just accept that no matter who you are or how much you make, awkward money moments are bound to happen. By staying mum, you're letting unnecessary tension build up in your relationships.

We've all been in situations where these personal issues arise: helping out a family member, pricey obligatory vacations, expensive group gift giving, and plain old awkward moments. Whether your friend wants you to invest in her new company, your uncle needs help paying for his children's college educations, or your sibling is really struggling, I've found that the key to dealing with these situations is to be honest.

If you're in a position where you want to and can (based on your, ahem, financial plan), great. But do so with *very* clear communication and expectations. Sometimes putting a simple document together saves a lot of headache later on.

On the other hand, if you're not in a position to help (and I'm aware that most people are really juggling their own financial to-dos), you may have to flat-out say no to something. When you do so, just be sure to emphasize that your decision isn't about him or her but your own financial needs. Blame the need to save for your down payment. Blame the fact that you don't yet have 529 plans for your kids. Blame me for giving you this advice in the first place. Whatever you say, just make the refusal about you, not them.

Don't Be That Money-Toxic Person

To be sure that *you're* not the one making people financially uncomfortable, I suggest being open and sensitive to other people's situations. This really comes down to being as thoughtful as possible. Some rules of thumb: When you're eating out in a group, always pick a cheaper restaurant. If you're planning a vacation, crowd-source ideas from everyone, as that alone will give you a good idea of what people are thinking moneywise. If you're in a real bind, recognize that when you ask for money help, you don't know what's happening on the insides of other people's wallets.

MONEY MIC: *The Mistake That Plunged My Credit Score 200 Points*

It was just before the housing market crashed in 2008, when a close friend decided to make the leap from renting to home ownership. Like myself, she was a single mom. We had known each other since grade school. We talked on the phone daily and had over twenty years of friendship between us.

When, in the eleventh hour, the bank told her she needed a co-signer in order to close on the property, I said I would do it. It was a knee-jerk reaction to help a friend.

I was self-employed and knew the repercussions of co-signing . . . sort of. But I didn't fully investigate exactly what would happen if she missed a payment. The plan was that she would refinance her home after a year of payments and get a new loan without me on it.

Everything went well for the first year. Unfortunately, the market was beginning to crumble. Before the real estate crash, banks were handing out refis like candy, but when my friend bought her home in 2009 they had started tightening their belts. She was unable to refinance me off her loan.

It wasn't until the fall of 2009, when I was thinking about getting satellite television, that I checked my credit report and discovered $10,000 in past due payments. My friend had missed not one, not two, but three mortgage payments! My credit score plummeted from over 800 to the low 600s when she defaulted on her mortgage. I was embarrassed and ashamed about the multitude of letters I received from my creditors telling me they were cutting *off my line of credit. Basically, I was left with no credit, no access to more credit, and a horrible credit score.*

I still don't know what happened—even while she was missing her payments, we were talking on the phone nearly every day, and it never came up. Whenever we talk about her delinquency, she's apologetic, but has never tried to justify it.

Her lack of communication and honesty destroyed our friendship. She wasn't forthcoming when she realized she was in trouble, and she wasn't honest about her ability to pay. Today, we barely speak unless it has to do with the house (which I've never even seen, as I live in Los Angeles while she and her house are in New Jersey).

As it stands, she hasn't made a mortgage payment in more than a year and owes almost $30,000. We owe this amount. Cosigning makes me just as liable. I've learned the lesson that you never want to put your financial livelihood in someone else's hands. And when you cosign, that's exactly what you do.

—Sibylla, 42, Los Angeles, CA "

Protect Yourself from . . . the Crazies

(aka Identity Thieves)

Long before I founded LearnVest, I once caught a bad case of credit-card fraud on one of my accounts. Because I was actively monitoring my transactions, one day I suddenly noticed charges from Barcelona, Paris, London, and Vienna—all charged in one day! (While I move fast, I'm not *that* fast.) I called up my bank to report it and was refunded immediately.

I was incredibly lucky to have caught it so quickly, especially since I noticed it en route to the airport, where I was catching a plane for an international trip. If I hadn't noticed it, the bank likely would have put a hold on my card and I would have found myself abroad with no money and a mess to clean up.

Chances are, you have a horror story of your own. For twelve years in a row, identity theft has been the top consumer complaint to the Federal Trade Commission—in 2011 there were 279,156 identity-theft complaints filed![7] There are a lot of lousy people out there who would love to steal your identity and your money. When you leave the house in the morning, you wouldn't leave your front door wide open with a big sign on it saying, "Rob me," would you? Well, that's essentially what you're doing if you don't take steps to protect yourself from identity thieves.

My Tips to Theft-Proof Yourself

1   **Take a daily Money Minute.** You already know this is critical for staying on budget, but it's also important because tracking each and every transaction is the only way to spot fraudulent ones you never made. If you find something questionable, dispute it online or call up your bank immediately and ask to speak to its fraud or identity-theft division. In addition, check your credit report regularly at AnnualCreditReport.com and CreditKarma.com to spot and correct any mistakes promptly (so they don't ding your credit!).

2   **Strengthen your passwords.** I know you're smart enough to avoid using silly passwords like "password123," or your name plus your birth date. But as hackers are getting more sophisticated, so should your passwords. Choose a password that no one but you could figure out, use different passwords for different accounts, and change up all your passwords *at least once a year.* (Set up a calendar reminder!) Keep one super cryptic password—the longer the better, no real words, and using a mix of letters and numbers— for sensitive accounts (meaning any account through which a financial transaction might occur) and another password for all your social-network accounts and other sites you may frequent. **Be sure to password-protect your computer *and* phone** so the random person who finds your iPhone in the back of a cab can't wire money straight out of your iPhone bank-account app.

3 **Use a credit card rather than a debit card for online shopping.** Credit cards have more consumer-friendly rules about your liability if fraud is detected. The max you'll be responsible for with a credit card is $50, versus $500 for a fraudulent debit-card transaction.

4 **Don't *ever* shop on an open network.** There are clues that show you exactly when something is secure: Make sure to spot the *s* in the website URL ("http" is not necessarily secure, while "https" should be). And look for the padlock symbol 🔒 to the far right of the URL and at the bottom of your screen. As you'd expect, a closed lock = secure.

5 **Mind your documents.** Sensitive documents you no longer need should be shredded. Don't throw anything with personal or identifying information in your trash. (If you think identity thieves are above fishing through your trash, think again.) A good litmus test when deciding whether to shred or not is whether you would share the info with a stranger: Your address? Probably fine. Your Social Security number? Absolutely not. For sensitive documents you plan to keep, make sure they're under lock and key. Safe-deposit boxes exist for a reason!

FEARLESS LESSON *Be Aware*

With all that said, **I don't think you need identify-theft insurance or overpriced tools that promise to alert you to theft.** Follow these steps and you're as protected as any of us can be. At the end of the day, there are people out there who will try to take advantage of you and throw you off track financially. The best you can do is be aware and have the proper systems in place to protect yourself.

What You've Accomplished

✓   Determined what you can negotiate in your employment contract

✓   Talked to your partner about finances and decided how to manage your money together

✓   Identified your money-toxic family and friends and learned how to handle them

✓   Made sure to protect yourself from identity thieves

Questions for Your Expert

If you still have questions about anything we've covered in this section, write them here and then go to www.learnvest.com/financiallyfearless for answers.

I still don't understand . . .

_____

_____

Where do I find . . .

Talk to an

LV

Expert

_____

_____

What should I do about my . . .

_____

_____

Examples:

My partner avoids the money talk at all costs. How do I start the conversation?

How often should I try to negotiate my salary? Is there a recommended time interval?

I was a victim of identity theft a while back. How do I make sure there aren't any lingering consequences I'm just not aware of?

PROTECT YOURSELF

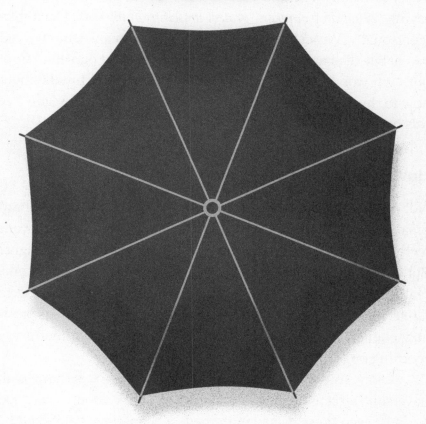

from

YOU

Yes, you heard me right. At this point in the book you may be saying, *What do you mean "protect myself from myself"?* Don't take it personally: We *all* have our bad habits and money demons. And bad habits die hard. That's why we need to protect ourselves from our own worst impulses. In this chapter I'm going to talk about how to thwart the bad habits you identified way back in Step 1 of this book.

How to Break Habits

Not convinced of the power of habit? To show yourself how hard breaking even a little, insignificant habit can be, try brushing your teeth every night with your nondominant hand. Tough, right? But observe how much easier it gets over time. At the same time, realize how easy it is to take on a new *bad* habit. According to Gretchen Rubin, author of *The Happiness Project*, two days is probably enough to form a bad habit, like getting a doughnut every morning on the way to work.[1]

Okay, so that's a silly example, but the point is that we all have subconscious habits we don't even think about. The good news is, even these deeply ingrained, subconscious habits can be changed! And the payoff will be huge: changing your habits can do what white-knuckling and willpower can't.

So how long will it take to undo your bad money habits? A serious 2009 study in the *European Journal of Social Psychology* looked into the difficulty of forming a habit like eating a piece of fruit with lunch or running for fifteen minutes a day. It found that different people had different time lines. For some the good new habits took only eighteen days. For others, 254 days! The study's ultimate conclusion was that on average **changing habits takes sixty-six days.**[2] So give yourself at least two months of daily practice to make your new habits automatic. I know that sounds daunting, but what's a couple of months to develop good habits that will stick with you **for life?**

In his definitive book *The Power of Habit*, Charles Duhigg explains how habits are formed and how to change them. He says that to figure out the roots of your bad habits you have to look at both the *cue*, or trigger, for the activity and the *reward* it's providing you.[3]

So if you're spending, say, $5 on a brioche every day at 4:00 p.m., you should figure out if you are being cued by actual hunger or by the simple fact that the clock has struck 4:00 and you're bored at work. Likewise, you should look at whether your body actually needs a brioche at that moment or whether the true reward is taking a break from work at that moment and just getting out of the office. Maybe you should just walk around the block instead and save $25 a week, $100 a month, $1,200 a year (not to mention thousands of empty calories!).

Duhigg also says that you need to build in mini rewards to create new habits. So if you are planning to start saving 5 percent of your paycheck every Friday afternoon, do something little right after the deposit hits to reward yourself, like treating yourself to a cupcake or going to happy hour with a friend. It's really hard to save without a little instant gratification, so build treats into your savings plan.

Your Bad Habits

To abolish your bad money habits once and for all, let's pick the three worst issues you identified in Step 1.

Recognize the difficulty level of your habit. It may be easy to switch from coffee to decaf (once you get past the withdrawal headaches) but not so easy to stop racking up credit-card debt, for example. So be sure to rank your bad habits on a scale of 1 to 5. Now write down what generally triggers that behavior and a way of avoiding that trigger. Then the fun part: specify how you'll reward yourself every time you manage to avoid or deflect that trigger. Make the plans tighter and the rewards greater accordingly!

Example of a Common Bad Money Habit

1. **PROBLEM:** Going out for expensive meals with friends.
2. **DIFFICULTY LEVEL:** 3—it's become central to your social life, even though it's not within your budget.
3. **TRIGGER:** Going to nice restaurants is your go-to when you spend time with your best friends. You like to catch up regularly, so it's part of the equation of seeing them.
4. **PLAN:** Research some alternatives that you can all enjoy—like less expensive spots or eating in more regularly instead.
5. **REWARD:** You do value eating out, so on a more special occasion, you can plan a nice dinner at a restaurant you've all been dying to try.

What's your bad money habit?

✓ Write it down

1. Problem: _____

2. Difficulty level: _____

Rate the difficulty level of fixing this problem on a scale of 1 to 5. An example of a 1 might be taking a new route home from work that doesn't take you past a shop where you frequently overspend. A 3 might be going to HR and asking them to put an extra 1 percent of your paycheck into your retirement account. A 5 could be getting on the same page with your partner about a bucket that's a perennial problem for your budget. Given how much my husband loves restaurants, in my case a 5 would be sorting out a plan with him for how we can avoid breaking our budget by eating out.

3. Trigger: _____

Figure out why you're doing it. What's the cue/trigger for this habit (time of day, place, emotion, presence of specific people, preceding behavior that has become ritualized)? For me it's overspending whenever I'm in certain stores.

4. Plan: _____

Give yourself a challenge. What's your plan for an alternative routine?

5. Reward: _____

Create a system that will make you want to follow through. What reward will you give yourself for achieving the new routine?

Bad Money Habit

1. Problem: _____

2. Difficulty level: _____

3. Trigger: _____

4. Plan: _____

5. Reward: _____

---

1. Problem: _____

2. Difficulty level: _____

3. Trigger: _____

4. Plan: _____

5. Reward: _____

When it comes to making positive change in your life, everyone's time line is different. Maybe you'll revamp your life this weekend and never look back. Maybe you'll change your habits one by one, until finally it all suddenly clicks. The tools are all here. The sooner you get started taking control of your money, the better, but remember, it's never too late.

Being smart about money is an ongoing process. And it requires constant and conscious behavioral change. *Wanting* to get in tip-top financial shape is not enough on its own—you have to create healthy habits that do much of the work for you. That's why this book (and supplemental tools) cover 360 degrees of your life. I've given you tangible challenges you can achieve. You should now have a goal of financial fearlessness in sight and the tools to make the goal a reality.

What You've Accomplished

✓   Identified your habits that hurt you financially

✓   Came up with a game plan to break your bad habits

Questions for Your Expert

If you still have questions about anything we've covered in this section, write them here and then go to www.learnvest.com/financiallyfearless for answers.

I still don't understand . . .

_____

_____

Where do I find . . .

_____

_____

What should I do about my . . .

_____

_____

Talk to an

LV

Expert

Examples:

How do I decide if the habit is "bad" enough for me to get rid of it?

I've tried to break bad money habits in the past, but it just doesn't stick. How do I truly hold myself accountable?

PAY IT FORWARD

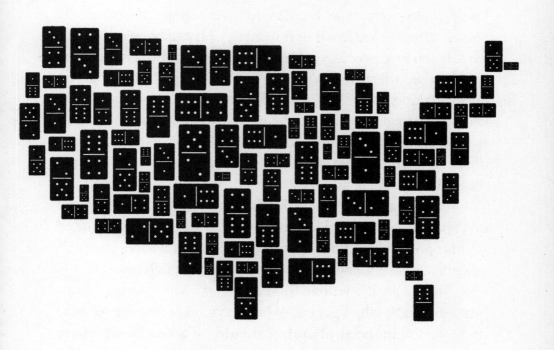

I've said it a million times, but I'll say it again: money is a lifeline. I wish that weren't true, but it is, for every single person on the planet. Whether we like it or not, money plays a huge role in our lives. If you love people, you're going to want to travel around the world to see them. If you're sick, you're going to want the best doctors taking care of you. If you have a baby, you will want to do everything to give your child the world. And like it or not, money is what makes these things possible. It's what gives you the freedom to **live your richest life.** This isn't the rehearsal. We're living the main show, here and now.

That means that *now* is the time to get good at money. You don't have to be a whiz. But you do need to take what you learned in this book and put it into practice. I hope that it saves you from anxiety and stress, and **that it brings you so much joy.**

That's why I've written this book, that's why I started Learn-Vest, and that's why I get out of bed *every single morning* eager to go to work. **Financial planning should be accessible to every single American.** Because money is *vital* to our ability to live our best lives. Now get out there, and go live yours.

So let's . . .

Start a Movement Together

Throughout this book, we've spent a lot of time focusing on ourselves. So let's remember to also focus on one another. We're in a tough spot as a nation. There's a student-debt bubble, crazy high credit-card debt, and thousands of people with underwater homes. **This nonsense has to stop.** This isn't magic. It's math. We as a country have to stop feeling ashamed about money and start taking control. We have the power to right the sinking ship!

This isn't just a book. It's the start of a movement. I encourage you to join in. Remember, finance should not be another F word. It should be something we talk about with our partners at the grocery store, with our friends at dinner parties, and with our mentors on coffee dates. We have to get rid of the sense of shame and anxiety around money if we—as individuals and as a nation—are going to make serious progress.

You've put in the time to get your budget in amazing shape. You're in control of your finances. You're on the road to living your richest life. And hopefully along the way you've learned that money isn't the enemy—**it's your lifeline.** It's time that we *all* stop feeling bad about money and see it for what it is: **a tool to start creating a positive change—in our lives and in the lives of those around us.** So spread the word. Share this book and the lessons you've learned with a friend—or with lots of friends.

So my parting words are a challenge. Since we are all stressing over this topic, share this information with a family member or best friend. I truly believe that once we begin to talk openly about money, together we can create a more secure, more responsible, more prosperous world.

The New Book Club Is . . . A LearnVest Club

We have weight-loss groups, running clubs, Tupperware parties, book clubs, Stella & Dot parties. Why not make financial fearlessness a social event, too? I feel so strongly about the value of this that if you get ten readers together, I will provide a LearnVest expert to call in to your first meeting and help kick things off (and that expert may even be me!).

① Get the Word Out
Invite your friends, your neighbors, your cousins, your best friends, your church members, your book club, anyone in your life you feel could benefit.

② Register Your LearnVest Club
Sign your club up at www.learnvest.com/financiallyfearless. Once you've signed up ten+ people, we'll schedule a time with one of our LearnVest experts for the kickoff meeting.

③ Open It Up
You want your guests to feel at ease so they can openly discuss their money worries, goals, and triumphs. As guests arrive, let everyone chat, catch up, and introduce themselves if necessary. Along the way, encourage guests to share their financial aspirations with the group (the exercises in "Groundwork: Your Money Mind-set" are the perfect way to dive in!).

Take the Next Step

At LearnVest's headquarters in New York City, we have our core company values painted on the wall. There is one in particular I want to share with you: **"We're tough because we care."** At LearnVest we hold you accountable. That's our job.

Now that you've finished this book, I'm sure you have tons of questions related to your unique situation. So put your hand up and ask for help. You bought this book to make a change, so let's do it.

Because this book is an investment in your richest life, we're investing in you, too.

Don't forget my gift to you: a $50 credit to speak with a LearnVest Program expert.

I am a firm believer in making financial planning a reality for everyone, no matter where they are on their journey to financial well-being. I even go so far as believing financial planning should be a civil right given its consequences. To take advantage of this offer, go to www.learnvest.com/financiallyfearless today.

Finally, because I'm on a serious mission to change this country, please share your own success stories and thoughts with me at fearless@learnvest.com. I'm always here.

Now go and build your richest life!

Notes

The F Word

1. Jim Forsyth, "More Than Two-Thirds in U.S. Live Paycheck to Paycheck—Survey," Reuters, September 19, 2012.

2. Joseph Pisani, "More Upper-Income Workers Living Paycheck to Paycheck," CNBC.com, September 16, 2009.

3. Carrie Yodanis and Sean Lauer, "Managing Money in Marriage: Multilevel and Cross-National Effects of the Breadwinner Role," *Journal of Marriage & Family* 69, no. 5 (December 2007): 1307–25.

4. This budget division appeared in Elizabeth Warren and Amelia Warren Tyagi's book *All Your Worth: The Ultimate Lifetime Money Plan* (New York: Free Press, 2006).

Step1: Where You Are Right Now

1. Brad Klontz et al., "Mind over Money: Money Beliefs and Financial Behaviors: Development of the Klontz Money Script Inventory," *Journal of Financial Therapy* 2, no. 1 (2011).

2. Brad Klontz, "The Big Lie About Personal Finance," Mind over Money, January 13, 2010, www.psychologytoday.com.

Groundwork: Your Money Mind-set

1. Klontz et al., "Mind over Money."

2. Ibid.

3. Ibid.

4. Joan D. Atwood, "Couples and Money," *American Journal of Family Therapy* 40 (2012): 1–19.

5. Michal Grinstein-Weiss et al., "Parental Transfer of Financial Knowledge and Later Credit Outcomes Among Low- and Moderate-Income Homeowners," *Children & Youth Services Review* 33, no. 1 (January 2011): 78–85.

6. Joyce Serido et al., "Financial Parenting, Financial Coping Behaviors, and Well-being of Emerging Adults," *Family Relations* 59 (October 2010): 453–64.

7. Dan Galai and Orly Sade, "The 'Ostrich Effect' and the Relationship Between the Liquidity and the Yields of Financial Assets," Hebrew University of Jerusalem, July 2003.

8. David Futrelle, "Your Emotions Can Cost You Money," interview with George Loewenstein, *Money* 40, no. 8 (September 2011).

9. "25 Ways to Waste Your Money," Kiplinger.com, March 2011, www.kiplinger.com/printslideshow.php?pid=9956&img=no.

10. Stephen E. G. Lea, Paul Webley, and Catherine M. Walker, "Psychological Factors in Consumer Debt: Money Management, Economic Socialization, and Credit Use," *Journal of Economic Psychology* 16, no. 4 (December 1995): 681–701, www.sciencedirect.com/science/article/pii/0167487095000134.

11. Carlin Flora, "How to Get over Status Anxiety," September 1, 2005, www.psychologytoday.com.

12. Keith Randolph, *The Truth About Creative Visualization* (St. Paul, Minn.: Llewellyn, 2002).

13. Gail Matthews, "Goals Research Summary," Dominican University, www.dominican.edu.

14. iGolu.com.

Running Your Numbers

1. Liz Weston, *Your Credit Score: How to Improve the 3-Digit Number That Shapes Your Financial Future* (Upper Saddle River, N.J.: FT Press, 2011), pp. 3–5.

2. Statistics from the U.S. Census, the Federal Reserve's Aggregate Revolving Consumer Debt Survey, and the Survey of Consumer Finances are helpfully crunched at NerdWallet.com: "American Household Credit Card Debt Statistics Through 2012," February 2013, www.nerdwallet.com/blog/credit-card-data/average-credit-card-debt-household/.

3. Employee Benefit Research Institute, "The 2012 Retirement Confidence Survey: Job Insecurity, Debt Weigh on Retirement Confidence, Savings," EBRI Issue Brief #369, March 2012, www.ebri.org/publications/ib/index.cfm?content_id=5017&fa=ibDisp.

4. Richard Wiseman, *59 Seconds: Think a Little, Change a Lot* (New York: Knopf, 2009).

Step 2: Your 50/20/30 Program

1. See Elizabeth Warren and Amelia Warren Tyagi, *All Your Worth: The Ultimate Lifetime Money Plan* (New York: Free Press, 2006).

2. Jim Forsyth, "More Than Two-Thirds in U.S. Live Paycheck to Paycheck—Survey," Reuters, September 19, 2012.

The 50: Essentials

1. "Housing Expenditures That Exceed 30 Percent of Household Income Have Historically Been Viewed as an Indicator of a Housing Affordability Problem," www.census.gov/housing/census/publications/who-can-afford.pdf.

2. U.S. Energy Information Administration Independent Statistics and Analysis, "Average Monthly Residential Electricity Consumption, Prices, and Bills by State," December 6, 2011, www.eia.doe.gov.

3. Allison Casey, "Stop Paying for Energy You Aren't Using," Energy.gov, January 6, 2009.

4. Sarah Goorskey, Kitty Wang, and Andrew Smith, "Home Energy Briefs: #8 Kitchen Appliances," Rocky Mountain Institute, 2004, www.rmi.org.

5. California Energy Commission, "Winter Time Energy Saving Tips," www.consumerenergycenter.org/tips/winter.html.

6. Ibid. Savings of $7 per month total $84 per year; www.fpl.com /residential/energy_saving/resources_tips/top_tips.shtml.

7. Timothy W. Martin, "Frugal Shoppers Drive Grocers Back to Basics," *Wall Street Journal,* June 24, 2009.

8. Martin Lindstrom, "The Race to Map Shopping DNA," Fan of the Consumer, September 30, 2011, www.martinlindstrom.com.

9. Stephanie Clifford, "At Stores, Making 5 for $5 a Bigger Draw Than 1 for $1," *New York Times,* July 17, 2011.

10. Marketing Science Institute as reported on CBSnews.com, February 18, 2010.

11. Assumes 8 percent annual interest rate, compounding monthly for thirty-three years. Ongoing contributions of $104 monthly. Does not account for inflation.

12. Brian McKenzie and Melanie Rapino, *Commuting in the United States: 2009* (September 2011), American Community Survey Reports, ACS-15, U.S. Census Bureau, Washington, DC.

The 20: Your Future

1. Assumes you begin work in your twenties and retire in your sixties with no other source of income and no independent wealth.

2. McGraw-Hill has a good chart in its online learning center expressing the value of your dollar at various interest rates over various periods of time. McGraw-Hill Higher Education, "Appendix: The Time Value of Money: Future Value and Present Value Computations," 2007, http://highered.mcgraw-hill.com.

3. CNN Money, "More Americans Delaying Retirement Until Their 80s," http://money.cnn.com.

4. "The Face of Personal Finance," A LearnVest & Chase Blueprint Study, http://5684-learnvest.voxcdn.com/wp-content/uploads/2011/03/100912_white -paper.pdf.

5. "Historical Annual Returns for the S&P 500 Index—Updated

Through 2011," Jim's Finance and Investment Blog, June 30, 2012, http://financeandinvestments.blogspot.com.

6. Inflation assumption from the U.S. inflation calculator.

7. Inflation assumption based on average inflation rate from 1913 to 2013 (about 3.3 percent), available at www.minneapolisfed.org.

8. Assumes initial investment of $1,000, forty-year period of growth, and a 5 percent annual rate of return and 3 percent rate of annual inflation.

9. "Majority of Americans Do Not Have Money Available to Meet an Unplanned Expense," National Foundation for Credit Counseling, www.nfcc.org, July 2011.

10. "99 Weeks: When Unemployment Benefits Run Out," CBSNews.com, October 25, 2010.

11. Amy Traub and Catherine Ruetschlin, "The Plastic Safety Net: 2012," Demos.org, May 22, 2012.

12. "American Household Credit Card Debt Statistics Through 2012," www.nerdwallet.com.

13. Charles Duhigg, *The Power of Habit* (New York: Random House, 2012).

14. Lorrin M. Koran et al., "Estimated Prevalence of Compulsive Buying Behavior in the United States," *American Journal of Psychiatry* 163, no. 10 (October 1, 2006): 1806–12.

15. April Lane Benson, ed., *I Shop Therefore I Am: Compulsive Buying and the Search for Self* (Lanham, Md.: Jason Aronson, 2000).

16. User Interface Engineering, "E-Commerce White Paper: What Causes Customers to Buy on Impulse?," February 4, 2002, www.uie.com.

17. "Tablets and Smartphones May Increase UK Consumer Impulse Buys by Up to £1.1 Billion per Year, Indicates Rackspace Retail Research," Rackspace.com, September 20, 2012, www.rackspace.co.uk.

18. Drazen Prelec and Duncan Simester, "Always Leave Home Without It: A Further Investigation of the Credit-Card Effect on Willingness to Pay," *Marketing Letters* 12, no. 1 (February 2001): 5–12, http://link.springer.com.

19. Helen Colby and Gretchen Chapman, "Don't Break the $100 Bill: Large Bills Promote Savings Behavior," unpublished, Medical Decision Making Lab, Rutgers University, www.rci.rutgers.edu.

20. Nerd Wallet, "Avoid Overdraft Fees by Opting Out of Overdraft Protection," November 4, 2010, www.learnvest.com.

21. Creditcards.com, "2012 Survey of Balance Transfer Cards Shows Offers Getting Better," January 19, 2012, www.foxbusiness.com.

22. www.nbcnews.com/business/balance-transfers-boon-credit-card-holders-1C6375831.

23. Accurate as of June 2013, Credit Card Screener, www.marketwatch.com.

24. For example, Green Path Debt Solutions (www.greenpath.com) charges a $50 monthly fee.

25. "Where Is the Best Place to Invest $102,000—in Stocks, Bonds, or a College Degree?" HamiltonProject.org, June 2011.

26. Rod Ebrahimi, "The 4 Most Common Loan Problems and How to Fix Them," Forbes.com, May 8, 2012.

27. Ibid.

28. Catherine Rampell, "Why Tuition Has Skyrocketed at State Schools," *New York Times,* March 2, 2012.

29. "Half of Recent College Grads Underemployed or Jobless, Analysis Says," Associated Press, April 23, 2012.

30. U.S. Department of Education, "First Official Three-Year Student Loan Default Rates Published" (press release), Ed.gov, September 28, 2012.

31. Andrew Martin and Andrew W. Lehren, "A Generation Hobbled by the Soaring Cost of College," *New York Times,* May 12, 2012.

32. Direct subsidized or unsubsidized Stafford loans have a six-month grace period, and Perkins loans have a nine-month grace period; www .studentloanborrowerassistance.org.

33. For more information visit www.studentaid.ed.gov.

34. Better Homes and Gardens Real Estate, "Next Generation of Homebuyers Are Knowledgeable, Responsible and Savvy According to New Better Homes and Gardens Real Estate Survey" (press release), October 22, 2012, www .bhgrealestate.com.

35. Kevin Quealy and Archie Tse, "Is It Better to Buy or Rent?" *New York Times,* 2012.

36. U.S. Department of Housing and Urban Development, Office of Policy Development & Research, "Untangling the Sources of Mortgage Closing Costs," Research Works 5, no. 8 (September 2008), www.huduser.org.

37. Keith Jurow, "Here's How Widespread Mortgage Fraud Created the Housing Bubble," Business Insider, May 18, 2010.

38. Mark Thoma, "Investor Speculation and the Housing Bubble," Economist's View, December 5, 2011.

39. www.huffingtonpost.com/2011/03/25/how-missing-workers-are -d_n_840570.html.

40. U.S. Department of Agriculture, "A Child Born in 2011 Will Cost $234,900 to Raise According to USDA Report" (press release), June 14, 2012, www .usda.gov.

41. www.cbsnews.com/8301-505144_162-37042296/raising-children-costs -between-286000-and-476000/.

42. Jane Walsh, "Extend Family Leave to All Workers," CNN.com, February 6, 2013.

43. http://denmark.angloinfo.com/healthcare/pregnancy-birth/leave -benefits/.

44. Katy Hall and Chris Spurlock, "Paid Parental Leave: U.S. vs. the World," Huffington Post, February 4, 2013.

45. The day-care center and home day-care numbers are from the National Association of Child Care Resource and Referral Agencies (NACCRRA) 2012 Report of Child Care Aware of America: www.naccrra.org/. The au pair and nanny costs are courtesy of aupairinamerica.com and nannies4hire.com.

46. Tracy Jan, "Fifty Thousand Dollars," *Boston Globe,* March 28, 2010.

47. Ron Lieber, "Saving for College: 18 Years in the Making," *New York Times,* April 14, 2009.

48. College Board, "Average Published Undergraduate Charges by Sector, 2012–13," collegeboard.org.

49. Charles Blaich, one of the researchers and the director of inquiries at the Center of Inquiry in the Liberal Arts at Wabash College and the Higher Education Data Sharing Consortium, quoted in Scott Jaschik, "Not Getting What You Paid For," *Inside Higher Education,* January 25, 2013.

50. U.S. Department of Labor, Bureau of Labor Statistics, "Economic News Release: Consumer Price Index Summary," www.bls.gov/news.release/cpi.nr0.htm.

51. College Board Advocacy and Policy Center, Annual Survey of Colleges; National Center for Education Statistics (NCES), Integrated Postsecondary Education Data System (IPEDS), October 2012, http://trends.collegeboard.org /college-pricing/figures-tables/published-prices-national#Tuition and Fee and Room and Board Charges over Time.

52. College Board Advocacy and Policy Center, "Figure 3: Average Aid per Full-Time Equivalent (FTE) Student in 2011 Dollars, 1973–74 to 2011–12," *Trends in Higher Education,* http://trends.collegeboard.org/student-aid/figures-tables /average-aid-full-time-equivalent-fte-student-2011-dollars-over-time.

53. General information on 529 plans can be found at www.sec.gov /investor/pubs/intro529.htm.

54. General information on prepaid plans can be found at www.sec.gov /investor/pubs/intro529.htm.

55. General information on Coverdell plans can be found at www.irs.gov /publications/p970/ch07.html.

56. www.usnews.com/education/best-colleges/paying-for-college /articles/2012/11/14/4-things-to-consider-when-changing-529-plan-beneficiaries.

57. "The MetLife Study of Caregiving Costs to Working Caregivers," Metlife Mature Market Institute, June 2011, www.metlife.com/mmi/research /caregiving-cost-working-caregivers.html?WT.ac=PRO_Pro2_NewMMI_5-18421 _T4297-MM-mmi&oc_id=PRO_Pro2_NewMMI_5-18421_T4297-MM-mmi#key findings.

58. Keith Randolph, *The Truth About Creative Visualization* (St. Paul, Minn.: Llewellyn, 2002).

59. "The Seduction of Day Trading," February 11, 2009, cbsnews.com.

60. The following instructions are intended as a general guideline when reviewing investment options on www.morningstar.com.

The 30: Your Lifestyle

1. Daniel Kahneman and Angus Deaton, "High Income Improves Evaluation of Life but Not Emotional Well-Being," Center for Health and Well-Being, Princeton University, August 4, 2010, www.pnas.org.

2. Robert Pagliarini, *The Other 8 Hours: Maximize Your Free Time to Create New Wealth & Purpose* (New York: St. Martin's Press, 2010).

3. Julianne Pepitone, "Why Your Cable Is Going to Cost You Even More," CNNMoney.com, January 9, 2010.

4. www.thedailybeast.com/newsweek/features/2010/the-beauty
-breakdown.html.

5. Annamaria Andriotis, "10 Things the Beauty Industry Won't Tell You," *SmartMoney*, April 20, 2011.

6. Based on an average number of meals out per week (3.2) and an average cost per meal ($35.65). "Zagat 2013 America's Top Restaurants Survey Reveals Meals Cooked at Home Surpass Meals Prepared Outside," November 14, 2012.

7. Martin Lindstrom, author of *Buyology: Truth and Lies About Why We Buy*, quoted in Carrie Sloan, "Girls Gone Wild: The Perils of Online Shopping," LearnVest Knowledge Center, September 6, 2011, www.learnvest.com.

8. Eric V. Copage, "How Online Retailers Read Your Mind," Gadgetwise, *New York Times*, December 22, 2009, http://gadgetwise.blogs.nytimes.com.

9. Anik Lalin et al., "Feeling Good About Giving: The Benefits (and Costs) of Self-Interested Charitable Behavior" (Harvard Business School Working Paper, 2009).

Protect Yourself from Life

1. "Life and Disability Insurance: What 20- and 30-Somethings Think," A LearnVest and Guardian Study, 5684-learnvest.voxcdn.com/wp-content/uploads/2013/01/Guardian-LearnVest_Whitepaper.pdf.

2. David U. Himmelstein et al., "Medical Bankruptcy in the United States, 2007: Results of a National Study," *American Journal of Medicine* 122, no. 8 (August 2009): 741–46.

3. Renee Y. Hsia et al., "Health Care as a 'Market Good'? Appendicitis as a Case Study," *Archives of Internal Medicine* 172, no. 10 (May 28, 2012): 818–19.

4. Arch G. Mainous III et al., "Impact of Insurance and Hospital Ownership on Hospital Length of Stay Among Patients with Ambulatory Care–Sensitive Conditions," *Annals of Family Medicine* 9, no. 6 (November/December 2011): 489–95.

5. U.S. Social Security Administration, "Social Security Basic Facts," February 7, 2013, www.ssa.gov/pressoffice/basicfact.htm.

6. These estimates come from a variety of national insurance providers and resources, including:

http://www.nationwide.com/car-insurance-discounts.jsp

http://www.esurance.com/discounts

http://www.statefarm.com/insurance/auto_insurance/discounts/auto-discounts.asp

http://www.forbes.com/sites/adamtanner/2013/08/14/data-monitoring-saves-some-people-money-on-car-insurance-but-some-will-pay-more

http://www.findmywayhome.com/special-interest/teacher-discount-auto-insurance

7. "Ownership of Individual Life Insurance Falls to 50-Year Low, LIMRA Reports," LIMRA, August 30, 2010, www.limra.com.

8. MetLife Mature Market Institute, "Market Survey of Long-Term Care Costs: The 2011 MetLife Market Survey of Nursing Home, Assisted Living, Adult Day Services, and Home Care Costs," October 2011, www.metlife.com.

9. Terri Sapienza, "Just to Be Safe, Load and Lock," *Washington Post,* January 11, 2007.

Protect Yourself from Others

1. Inflation assumption based on average inflation rate from 1913 to 2013 (about 3.3 percent), available at http://www.minneapolisfed.org.

2. Syble Solomon has a "Habitudes" deck, which includes the following goals: security, targeted goals, status, selfless, free spirit, and spontaneous, found at www.moneyhabitudes.com. Judith Stern Peck has cards in her book *Money and Meaning* (Hoboken, N.J.: Wiley, 2007) that include "Process Values," like reflective thinking, collaboration, hierarchy, inclusive values, exclusive values, dialogue, transparency, empowerment, and equality.

3. Catherine Rampell, "Money Fights Predict Divorce Rates," *New York Times,* December 7, 2009.

4. Ibid.

5. Allegra Zagami, "What's a Postnup and Who Should Get One?" *Fox News Magazine,* January 8, 2013.

6. "New Survey Reveals the Costs of Friendship," CouponCabin.com, July 18, 2012.

7. Federal Trade Commission statistics released February 28, 2012.

Protect Yourself from You

1. Gretchen Rubin, "Stop Expecting to Change Your Habit in 21 Days," *Psychology Today,* October 21, 2009.

2. P. Lally, C. H. M. van Jaarsveld, H. W. W. Potts, and J. Wardle, "How Are Habits Formed: Modelling Habit Formation in the Real World," *European Journal of Social Psychology* 40, no. 6 (October 2010): 998–1009.

3. Charles Duhigg, *The Power of Habit* (New York: Random House, 2012).

Index